GENERAL PATTON'S PRINCIPLES FOR LIFE AND LEADERSHIP

by

Porter B. Williamson

MSC, INC
Management & Systems Consultants, Inc.
Sun-University Station, #40457
Tucson, Arizona, 85718
USA

GEN. PATTON'S PRINCIPLES
For
FOR LIFE AND LEADERSHIP

Fourth Edition
27th Printing

Other books by the author:
Arizona Real Estate Laws
Arizona Property Tax Laws
Arizona Zoning and Subdivision Laws
Strength From Weakness
The Hammerhead Mission
The Abstainer Pill

Library of Congress Number - 88-81003
ISBN Numbers:
Quality paperback - 0-918356-06-7
Hardcover - 0-918356-07-5
Gift (padded cover) - 0-918356-08-3

Published by:
Management and Systems Consultants, Inc.
Sun-University Station, 40457,
Tucson, Arizona 85717
United States of America

Printed and manufactured in
The United States of America

CONTENTS

PREFACE

"God is truth" is an Old Testament principle which Gen. Patton followed. He spoke the truth when it was unpopular to speak truth. By his words and his actions he constantly attempted to get at the basic truth of every situation. He slapped the man who needed to be slapped. Ten years after the face slapping incident, this man admitted Gen. Patton had every right to give more severe discipline than a slap. Interviewed by a newspaper reporter, this man admitted, "Maybe if I had played it right I could have gotten home a lot sooner." Soldiers do not try to get home sooner when there is a war to be won.

Many readers who served with Gen. Patton may note that I have not listed all of his principles. Not all of his expressions resulted in some event which could be reported. It would be difficult to give examples for the following principles: "Every man is expendable, including generals, if the results are worth it!" "If we run out of food, we will eat the enemy or each other!" Gen. Patton often used the expression, "An ounce of sweat will save a gallon of blood!"

I regret that I cannot remember all of the phrases which Gen. Patton used. He was the king of all phrase makers. His barbs of truth sharpened the minds of every listener.

I have tried to imitate Gen. Patton's talent for using machine gun bursts of words. Between the short bursts of words, he would pause to let the troops enjoy a laugh or to absorb the full truth of his statement. When Gen. Patton spoke to the troops he held the attention of every soldier, and he said as much with his carefully timed silent periods as he did with his machine gun bursts of words. Many readers will puzzle over the absence of profanity in this book. No one could imitate Gen. Patton's profanity.

Several Patton authors called the General arrogant, foolhardy and flamboyant. No writer caught the importance of the pistols, the arrogant lectures, and the flamboyant actions as the carefully rehearsed and planned actions of a man who knew how to lead men into combat with the enemy and with death. No writer who called Gen. Patton foolhardy caught the importance of immediate pursuit of the retreating enemy. No writer caught the humility and the religion of Gen. Patton.

The first draft of this book was sent to Major General George S. Patton, the son, who returned the manuscript with only one word changed. He suggested that the principle, "Never listen to your fears" should be "Never take counsel of your fears." I knew he was correct. I had used "listen" in place of "counsel" for an easier word to understand. Many readers have written to confirm the incidents which I report about Gen. Patton.

I have great pride in the words of Mrs. Ruth Ellen Totten, the General's daughter, who said, "Your book is the best book about my father." Also, the opinion of Gen. Patton's son who said, "I know my father would be proud to have his principles sorted out by you."

WE CAN ALWAYS LEARN FROM EACH OTHER

I served **with** General George S. Patton, Jr. No man served **under** Gen. Patton; he was always serving **with** us. In truth, I still serve with Gen. Patton, and he continues to serve with me. He makes me take cold showers, he makes me take deep breaths, and he makes me pull in my bushel of blubber.

He served with me when the doctors told me I had terminal cancer. He told me, "Did you ever stop to think that death can be more exciting than life?"

When I fall he tells me, "The test of success is not what you do when you are on top. Success is how high you bounce when you hit bottom."

When I have a difficult decision to make, he tells me, "No decision is difficult to make if you will get all of the facts."

When I get scared, he says, "Never take counsel of your fears."

When I get angry and want to strike back in revenge, he orders, "Do not forget revenge belongs to God."

I will relate the Gen. Patton principles which I remember. Gen. Patton was a genius if a genius is a man with ideas thirty years ahead of the leaders of society. Gen. Patton combined the genius of a military leader with the talents of a religious scholar.

My first meeting with Gen. Patton was on a bridge over a small stream in South Carolina. It was a chilly afternoon in November, a few days before Pearl Harbor, in December of 1941. We were on maneuvers (war games) with the I Armored Corps. In a few months the I Armored Corps would have over fifty thousand men. In November, 1941, the I Armored Corps had a dozen officers and less than a hundred men in a Headquarters Company. The I Armored Corps had been authorized (created) in the mid-year of 1941 to coordinate the First and Second Armored Divisions of the United States Army. At full strength an armored division would have fifteen thousand men. In the few months since the I Armored Corps had been authorized, only a limited amount of weapons and equipment had been received. We did have an abundance of staff cars because the army staff cars were exactly the same as the civilian four-door sedans except for the GI drab color.

When our I Armored Corps was moved to South Carolina, we received orders that Gen. Patton's Second Armored Division would be under our command. Gen. Patton's reputation was so well known that our G-4 Supply Officer asked for an immediate transfer. This Regular Army Colonel was a competent and well trained officer. When he learned that he had to supply fuel and rations to Gen. Patton's Division, the Colonel said, "There is no way in the world fuel can be delivered to that "Hell on Wheels" Division. We do not have the trucks nor cans nor men! I am getting out of the I Armored Corps. I am not going to be made to look like a fool at this stage of my military career!"

"Hell on Wheels" was the name Gen. Patton had given his division to indicate their speed of travel. "Cans" were the usual five gallon gas cans now available in war surplus stores. Refueling an armored tank in the field required the five gallon cans be carried by soldiers. Gasoline and diesel tank trucks could not roll through the fields nor could tank trucks be exposed to aircraft attacks. The fuel was pumped (milked) into the five gallon cans from the tank trucks and carried by the men for several hundred yards to the tanks. Large trucks could not go

2

through the mud and fields as easily as the track laying tanks; however, the tanks were not permitted to park "bumper to bumper" to avoid being an easy target for planes.

With the transfer of our G-4 officer to Fort Knox, the task of keeping Gen. Patton supplied with fuel fell upon me, the only other G-4 Officer on the I Armored Corps Staff. As a first lieutenant, I could fail, as I was advised by our Chief of Staff. The failure would be based on my lack of military experience since I was a civilian reserve officer. Despite my lack of experience I was determined to do the best I could whether I failed or not.

As I think about the event now, thirty-five years later, I am certain that this Carolina war game was a maneuver to cause Gen. Patton to fail with the new things called "tanks." The old line officers in the infantry, field artillery and cavalry wanted to win all wars. The new tanks changed the ideas about how to win wars. The horse cavalry existed in name with few horses, but the old line officers continued to think horse tactics without any thought of using tanks. As Billy Mitchell pushed for the use of aircraft in war, Gen. Patton pushed for the use of armored tanks. One way to prove that tanks would fail in war would be to cut off Gen. Patton's gas and diesel fuel supplies.

I had a good relationship with our I Armored Corps Chief of Staff, the first officer in rank under the Commanding General. It was this senior Colonel who advised me that I could fail without causing any loss in efficiency points for my military file. I talked to the Chief of Staff about my authority as the G-4 Officer, how much money I could spend, and what procedures to follow. After many years of cutting money for defense, Congress in 1941 wanted to get money to the Army as fast as possible. We had more money than we could spend. With the help of the Chief of Staff I secured the proper papers to spend any amount of money necessary to get fuel to Gen. Patton's 2nd Armored Division. With this authorization, my impressive staff car and driver, I set out to do the best I could.

All of our fuel was in railroad tank cars in a city about seventy miles from the "combat" area. There was ample gasoline and diesel fuel, but the fuel was too far away. Since we didn't have the tank trucks, cans, nor men, the only way to solve the problem would be to move the fuel by rail.

With this plan in mind I picked up a driver, and we drove to the railroad center where our gas was located. I carried all of my papers into the railroad office to talk with the officials. In November of 1941, with the war raging in Europe, civilians would do anything to help with the war games. I asked that the tank cars be moved to the battle area and "spotted" (parked) on a railroad track that was higher than the land along the side of the railroad tracks. With the tank cars elevated, we could use gravity to fill the little five gallon cans and forget about needing "milkers" to pump the fuel into the cans. With luck we might be able to refuel the armored tanks directly from the railroad cars on a drive-up basis. There was a major problem. It was Saturday! No train crews were on duty to move the tank cars.

As I recall the conversation with the railroad officers, I can understand their attitude. They could not believe that a young first lieutenant could spend so much money. After several telephone calls, the officials said it could be done. Many little problems remained as major hurdles: over-time pay, approval of the train dispatchers in charge of the trains already on the tracks, a secretary to

4

type a large bundle of forms, and whether to type one form (bill of lading) for each tank car or one form for all of the tank cars!

I could type so I typed the forms for the railroad officials who told me what to type as they looked over my shoulder. While we waited for the train crew, we studied the railroad maps. I drew a circle around the area where we needed the fuel.

There were numerous calls to my boss, the Chief of Staff for the I Armored Corps. I wanted to be sure that moving the gas by rail did not break any of the war game rules. The Chief of Staff checked with the umpires for the war game, and we were "legal."

I did not leave the railroad office until the train crew was moving the tank cars out of the railroad yard and onto the main track. All other trains were to take the side-tracks and wait for the tank cars to pass. The railroad officials were kind and did not make an excessive charge for the special train crew. Finally, my driver and I left for the area where we hoped to find the train crew with the tank cars of gasoline and diesel fuel for the tanks and trucks.

Several hours later we met the train at the elevated track near a highway. The tank cars were parked about two hundred feet apart to make it easier for the armored tanks to pull in for refueling. There was sufficient gravity for the fuel to flow into the armored tanks without the use of any milking machines. Everything seemed perfect! A row of trees along the highway protected the refueling operation from easy vision from enemy aircraft. My new problem was how to get the information to Gen. Patton's Headquarters. Nothing would be gained if the 2nd Armored, the Hell on Wheels Division, did not know where the fuel was located.

We Can Always Learn From Each Other

I did not have any success in trying to reach Gen. Patton's Headquarters because they were not connected into any public telephone system.

In 1941 we did not have many short wave radios for our military vehicles. Most of the radios we had were usually in for repair due to the rough usage required by our war equipment. I did reach our Corps Headquarters and relayed the location of the gasoline. The instructions to the 2nd Armored Division had to be exact. The entire division would have to travel a narrow country road. It would be foolish to send twelve thousand men with tanks and trucks down a rural highway hunting for a row of tank cars. Gen. Patton's officers had to know exactly where the fuel was located.

Time was short. At midnight the 2nd Armored Division would be moving out for the attack. I could see that my plans would be a total failure if the 2nd Armored Division could not get the fuel. In November, darkness would come early! I was beginning to understand the reason the senior colonel wanted to be far away when the war games started. I could see that I would be charged with losing a large sum of money by putting fuel in a place where it could not be used.

I directed my driver to use country roads going towards the area where the 2nd Armored Division was reported to be. I wanted to find some troops wearing the colors of the 2nd Armored Division so I could find their headquarters. As we drove towards a small bridge I was happy to see a 2nd Armored tank, but I was disgusted because the tank was blocking the narrow bridge across a small stream I needed to cross. A grey-haired sergeant was in the turret of the tank. I judged the man to be a World War I sergeant who could be as stubborn as he was old. According to the war-game rules, armored tanks were not permitted to use any bridge. Tanks had to cross the streams in the water. If the tanks could not cross the stream, the engineers had to build a pontoon bridge. In war it was assumed that all bridges would be destroyed. I would read the rules to the Army sergeant and get him off the bridge.

Cooling my anger, I reasoned that before I ordered the sergeant off the bridge I should try to learn where the 2nd Armored Headquarters was located. If I made the sergeant angry, he would refuse to tell me anything. As I approached the bridge I saw a second tank was submerged in the water at the side of the bridge. Only the turret of the tank was out of the water. I studied the sunken tank as I approached the bridge.

"She's in deep!" a high pitched voice called. "The men got out and are safe!"

The old Army sergeant put on his helmet, and I saw two silver stars. Going into shock, I could see two silver stars on the tank. It was Gen. Patton who had called to me!

"Yes, sir!" I froze in place.

"Their speed was not high enough when they hit the water so they sunk! I'm sure they could have floated a bit if they had hit the water at top speed. We got to be able to cross this kind of stuff without bridges. It takes too much time to build a pontoon bridge for these little streams."

"Yes, sir!"

Gen. Patton continued to explain the proper way to maneuver a tank across a stream. Finally, he asked, "What outfit you with?"

"I Armored Corps, sir"

"Where in hell is the G-4? The Supply Officer? Where in hell is the fuel? I need gas and lots of it! I

7

understand fuel is a hundred miles away."

Gen. Patton continued to ask questions. At last, he called our former Supply Officer, known as G-4, by name and asked if I knew what the colonel planned to do about the fuel supply problem.

I answered, "He does not plan to do anything, sir."

"Then this war game will be over before it starts! I cannot move ten miles without gas." He continued to stress the need for fuel. Finally, he asked if I knew where the former G-4 Officer could be reached.

"He cannot be reached, sir. He is on his way to Fort Knox. He has transferred out of our I Armored Corps."

"Then who in hell is the G-4 for I Armored Corps?"

"I am, sir."

There was silence as Gen. Patton stared at me in amazement. He mumbled profanity and disappeared into his tank. I turned away and walked to my staff car. It was easy to see that Gen. Patton was disgusted that such a junior officer was in charge of his fuel problems. I was disgusted that I had not been permitted to explain where the fuel was located.

Before I reached the staff car, Gen. Patton called, "Lieutenant!"

I turned to see him jump from the tank with a bundle of maps in his hand.

"I'm Gen. Patton. I am the Commanding General of the 2nd Armored Division. We need diesel fuel and gas; lots of it! What's your name?"

I gave him my name.

Gen. Patton started with simple facts. "We've got a real problem here."

He spread his maps on the trunk of my staff car. Pointing on the map, he said, "Right here is where we expect Gen. Drum to be with his First Army. This is the enemy we have to destroy. Our problem is we have to cross several little streams like this one here in order to get into a position for a battle in this area. The problem is we do not have any fuel."

When I had a chance to speak, I said, "General, in the Armored Corps we do not have gas trucks, cans, nor men to move a hundred gallons of any type of fuel. There is no possible way we could supply fuel on the route which you have pointed out on your map. I am sorry to say that the only place we can get fuel to you is here." I pointed to the area where the tank cars were parked on the railroad tracks. We could not find the exact location on Gen. Patton's maps since his map did not show railroads.

"General, let me show you on my map where the gas is available." I reached into the car for my maps. My driver was sitting as stiff as a mummy. Every one was rigid when Gen. Patton was near.

As I unfolded my maps, Gen. Patton asked, "Where did you get that map?"

"From National Geographic," I answered.

"How?"

"I subscribe to the magazine. The maps come with the magazine."

Studying the map, he commented, "Your map is a hell of a lot better than mine! I have been using gas station maps. All of my military maps are out of date. None of my maps show the railroads!"

We compared maps. I was anxious to explain the facts about the location of the railroad tank cars but did not have a chance. I was a new military officer without much knowledge of the unwritten military rules, but I knew that two-star generals were not interrupted.

Gen. Patton continued to present the problem.

"Knowing the railroads I doubt that they would move the gas for a week. We need that gas now. Even if we could get the gas where you say . . . we are dry! But we could send trucks for a few thousand gallons . . . but we couldn't get the gas out of a tank car without milkers. All this would be in violation of the rules for these war games."

Gen. Patton paused and smiled, "But if . . . !"

It was my turn to smile! "General Patton, the fuel is on the railroad tracks right there now!" I pointed to the marks I had made on my map which had all of the railroads. "It is not in violation of the rules for the war games. Our I Armored Corps Chief of Staff checked this out with the war game umpires."

"But that railhead is off the main highways where we had planned to attack! Lieutenant, whose idea was it to move that gas by rail? Do you know that the tank cars are there and going to stay there? If we roll up there and get stranded dry without gas away from the battle area, we could look stupid, to say the least!"

"I just came from there! The railroad will not move the tank cars. I had the task of getting fuel to you and that is the only place I could see that we could make the fuel available. I have been assured that the tank cars will not be moved for a week."

"Can't be! This war game does not start until midnight tonight. You broke the rules by moving too early!"

"General, if it a is violation of the rules, it is not your fault because our Chief of Staff cleared everything. That fuel can be considered fuel which you could capture from the enemy!"

"Can we just go up there and tank-up? Are you sure we will not get in trouble with the war game umpires? Or the railroad?"

We Can Always Learn From Each Other

I explained the clearance from the umpires, the gravity-feed plan for the tank cars, the contract with railroad, and all of the facts that I had about the tank cars.

Gen. Patton took my map and opened it to full size on the top of the staff car. He was tall enough to use the top of the four-door sedan. I continued to hold the other maps on the trunk of the car. He drummed his fingers on the top of the car and mumbled, "No one would ever expect us to take a longer route. It is further, but we will have plenty of fuel. We will send a light force . . .. They would be able to return with enough fuel to . . .. In six hours . . .?"

Gen. Patton smiled and turned to me, "You son-of-a-bitch! You've done it! We can sure learn from each other! May I borrow your map? My old friend, Gen. Drum, will not even have a map showing where I am going to attack. Gen. Drum is the Commander of the Army against us, you know. He is an old friend, but I sure as hell would enjoy capturing him. It will prove tanks can win wars!"

I agreed to loan my map. Requests of a two-star general were not denied by a lieutenant.

He gave his gas station maps to me, saying, "Not a fair trade, but we got to move fast. Would you wait right here for a minute until I try to cross this stream? I want to be sure that our tanks can cross this kind of water without a pontoon bridge. Then, if I may, I would like to hitch-hike a ride with you to my headquarters. I have to get back as fast as possible to make a complete change in our battle plan!"

As we walked towards the bridge and Gen. Patton's tank, he said, "We can always learn from each other. You watch me cross this stream. You taught me that you reserve officers can come up with new ways to solve

11

problems. I'll show you how to get a tank across a small river!"

Gen. Patton ran towards his tank. I walked towards the bridge. At first I was disgusted he went into such detail about the fuel problem. I had been in the middle of that problem all day! I was amazed a two-star general would ask to hitch-hike a ride with a lieutenant. Most generals would have taken over my car and driver. It was also amazing to see a two-star general run!

ALWAYS DO EVERYTHING YOU ASK
OF THE MEN YOU COMMAND

Gen. Patton jumped onto the side of his tank and squeezed into the turret. The tank driver "buttoned up" by closing the front metal window of the tank so that water and bullets could not enter. When the driver was buttoned up, the man in the turret controlled the direction of the tank by pressure on the right or left shoulder of the driver. The speed of the turn was determined by the amount of pressure of the tank commander' foot on the driver's shoulder. Hard pressure on the right shoulder was an order to make a hard right turn.

This was not a good system, but the best we had been able to invent in 1941. When the driver was "buttoned up" he had a tiny periscope for his forward vision, but the area he could see outside the tank was a blur. Most of the time the man in the turret controlled the direction of the tank.

Gen. Patton's head popped out of the turret. The armored tank backed off of the bridge and into the weeds along the roadside ditch. When the tank had backed about a fifty yards from the bridge, the driver raced his engine to full speed. Gen. Patton braced his body against the iron sides of the turret. The tank tracks started throwing dirt into the air as the tank headed for the river. There was a great splash as the tank hit the water. The engine sputtered! I was sure there would be a wet general swimming out of the tank. The silver stars of the general's flag disappeared under the water. For a moment the tank floated on the water until the tank's tracks jammed into the mud on the other side of the stream. The engine continued to sputter, but the tank rolled up the bank. When the tank stopped, mud and water dripped from every nut and bolt.

Always Do Everything You Ask
Of The Men You Command

Gen. Patton's head disappeared again as he went into the tank. Suddenly he was out of the tank and running towards me.

I would learn later that Gen. Patton had followed one of his basic principles: "Always do everything you ask of the men you command." A slow attack on the river with a tank, and the tank would sink as the tank on the side of the bridge had done.

Within a few hours in the darkness of midnight, every tank of the 2nd Armored Division would cross that little river and several other small rivers!

On the drive to Gen. Patton's headquarters, he never gave a single instruction to my driver. I did not know which country road to take, but Gen. Patton did not give any orders to my driver. He would say, "Would you ask your driver to turn at the next road?" I did not need to repeat the instruction! The driver obeyed Gen. Patton's questions to me! I was in I Armored Corps which did not take any orders from the 2nd Armored Division, a lower military organization in the chain of command. Gen. Patton would not give any orders to my driver! When we reached Gen. Patton's headquarters, he thanked me for the maps and the ride and ran for his office tent. When I reached our Corps Headquarters, I was ordered back into the combat zone with a new driver. Drivers had to have sleep. Officers could sleep while the staff cars were moving. I never found any unit of the 2nd Armored Division that night nor the next morning. The "Hell on Wheels" division was living up to its name. I spent Sunday driving from town to town trying to find Gen. Patton's headquarters to arrange for a new railhead for fuel and rations.

Early Sunday afternoon Gen. Drum, the "enemy"

commander, drove into the combat zone to have photos taken for the newspapers and photo magazines. The war game was to last for ten days. Gen. Drum reasoned that the maneuvers would not get started until Monday morning. Sunday would be the day for both forces to prepare for the maneuvers on Monday. The photo-taking was a disaster for Gen. Drum, but a great day for the photographers.

As the photographers were shooting the action pictures of Gen. Drum riding into "combat" with his arms waving and shouting orders, an advance group of Gen. Patton's motorcycle riflemen roared into the area with all of their sirens screaming. Nothing in the war-game rules made any exceptions for captured generals. Gen. Drum was treated as any other prisoner of war; to the enjoyment of the news photographers. No amount of talking would move Gen. Patton's riflemen to release Gen. Drum!

When Gen. Patton arrived Gen. Drum asked not to be treated as a regular prisoner of war. Gen. Patton consented provided Gen. Drum would surrender his dress saber for the benefit of the photographers. Gen. Drum refused. Gen. Patton ordered his men to wrap Gen. Drum in toilet paper to indicate capture.

Gen. Drum protested that Gen. Patton's men were out of uniform because they were wearing civilian overcoats. Gen. Patton went into a rage accusing Gen. Drum of playing politics by having winter clothing and gasoline at a rail center seventy miles from the "war zone." Gen. Patton also asked in front of the media, "Have you briefed these men that you have an army of 196,000 opposing our army of only 99,000? How much politics are you playing in this war game?

Gen. Drum was silent and handed Gen. Patton his dress

saber which Gen. Patton returned after photos were taken. No photo of this capture appeared in the New York Times.

I learned of Gen. Drum's capture from a telephone operator who had a soft southern accent. She told me she had talked with a Gen. Drum who wanted to be released in "the worst way" from a prisoner of war camp. She said, "My, but that man was sure having a hissy-fit!"

Although the war game was over with the capture of Gen. Drum, I was busy day and night trying to get rations, supplies, and fuel relocated for the 2nd Armored Division. I changed from the staff car to a captured jeep. The jeep could go into the fields and wooded areas. Several nights later, completely exhausted, I returned to I Armored Corps Headquarters. Our Chief of Staff complimented me, saying, "Keeping Gen. Patton happy is not an easy assignment. He gave us all kinds of compliments for our moving fast enough to keep him supplied with gas and rations."

I went to my small-wall tent and fell on my cot in a cold chill. With four blankets I could not stop shaking. Our Corps Surgeon checked on me and piled on more blankets. The shaking and the chill stopped, but the Corps Surgeon wanted a patient to put in his new ambulance. He strapped me on a litter, MASH style, and sent me to a hospital. I never returned to I Armored Corps in South Carolina. With the capture of Gen. Drum the maneuvers ended. Gen. Patton had set the record clear that tanks could win wars!

When I rejoined I Armored Corps in a new building at Fort Knox, Kentucky, it was Sunday afternoon, and the radio was blaring something about enemy planes bombing Pearl Harbor. One of the senior officers on the staff said, "Those radio people will do anything to try to get people

16

excited enough to listen to'em. "

Our Intelligence Officer for the Corps suggested, "We knew that a Jap navy task force was in the Pacific. That news must be correct. I am sure we are in the war!"

Within a few days after the arrival of the I Armored Corps in Fort Knox, Kentucky, we were ordered to Fort Benning, Georgia. The 2nd Armored Division and Gen. Patton were stationed at Fort Benning. The rumors were getting stronger that Gen. Patton would be the new Commanding General of our Armored Corps. Gen. Charles Scott, our Commanding General, was several years past retirement age. We knew that Gen. Scott would be retired as soon as we had more officers on the staff. Many officers on our staff were alarmed that they might have to serve with Gen. Patton. Although my experience with Gen. Patton resulted in my going to the hospital for exhaustion and a cold chill, I had enjoyed working with Gen. Patton and his staff.

In 1976, thirty-five years after the Carolina maneuvers, I was watching a television interview of one of DR's advisors. I had forgotten about the refueling problem until I heard FDR's advisor comment, "The Carolina maneuvers of 1941 kept Gen. Drum from a high command in World War II. He was in line for the top command in Europe. Gen. Patton captured Gen. Drum on the first day of the war game. Drum accused Patton of buying gas from the local gas stations with his own money. Drum never recovered from his capture by Gen. Patton's men. I think he retired after he lost the Carolina war game in front of all of the news media."

Gen. Patton would never hesitate to use his own money to purchase fuel from local service stations if it had been possible to buy from service stations. However, heavy armored tanks could not use the roads to get to the local gas stations. No gas station would have had enough gas and diesel fuel for a division of armored tanks.

As I listened to the television interview, I remembered again of our suspicions of 1941 that the political military leaders had planned to make Gen. Patton and the tanks appear worthless in war. Their plan had failed.

A COMMANDER WILL COMMAND!

When Gen. Patton assumed a command there was an instant change throughout the entire organization. The command changed as if every man changed from 110 volt motivation to 440! Executive managers and psychologists lecture on how to exercise authority and to command men and women to gain an objective. Gen. Patton did not follow many of the usual principles of management. Psychologists would complain that Gen. Patton's principles failed to protect the ego of the person. Gen. Patton would answer that a dead soldier did not have any ego. Everything Gen. Patton did was to prevent his soldiers from being killed so that they could kill the enemy. Ego-building, face-saving, and all of the time consuming methods "begging" a worker to work cannot be used in time of war.

I will never forget Gen. Patton assuming command of I Armored Corps. I am grateful to the soldier who snapped a picture of the event! The photo is fuzzy but the straight line of Gen. Patton's 2nd Armored Division troops and our rag-tag group of staff members of I Armored Corps - all can be seen except the two stray dogs. It was January 15, 1942, a few weeks after Pearl Harbor on December 7. I Armored Corps had moved from Fort Knox to a bivouac (camp) in a pine tree grove on the edge of the main post of Fort Benning, Georgia. Our I Armored Corps was a hybrid military organization. Fort Benning was a standard-brand type of military organization, an infantry post. The I Armored Corps was a collection of men from the infantry, field artillery, and cavalry. In simple terms, the armored tanks did the work of the foot soldiers, used the big guns of the field artillery, and raced into combat at speeds that exceeded the speed of horses.

19

A Commander Will Command

Although Hitler was using tanks to destroy Europe, many of our infantry, field artillery and cavalry officers were not ready to let any new tank outfit take over their duties.

There was a dream among the cavalrymen that there would be a day when horses would return. Many of these horse-thinking officers held high positions of command in Washington. No tank outfit would be permitted to change the established military trunk-to-tail thinking of who would get the command positions to win the war. Most of the old line military officers wanted tanks to be in their command. Few leaders wanted a new Armored Force equipped with only tanks. Such a drastic step would change war from defense to offense.

Because we were a hybrid organization with our loud noisy tanks, we were removed from the main post area of Fort Benning. Another reason for us to be off the main post was that our track-laying tanks could destroy concrete and black-top roads. In our off-post area, our headquarters building looked like a small chicken house for laying hens. We lived in tents and used the pot-bellied stoves from World War I for heating our tents and our headquarters building.

We received orders from Washington that Gen. Patton would assume command of our I Armored Corps on the 15th day of January, 1942. No hour of the day was indicated on the order. Usually a new commanding general would arrive some time after the date for assuming command and would stroll into headquarters after he and his wife had moved their clothes and property into military quarters. All of our quarters were in tents including the quarters for the Commanding General - until Gen. Patton built a log cabin which was his home and our Officers' Club. The day after receiving the notice that Gen. Patton would assume command, we received an order from Gen.

A Commander Will Command

Patton.

The Gen. Patton order gave the same date and set the exact hour, eleven o'clock, that Gen. Patton would assume command. This second order provoked laughter from the older officers on the staff. It was unheard of for a new commander to set an exact hour for assuming command! Knowing of Gen. Patton's reputation, some of the older officers transferred to other organizations rather than serve with Gen. Patton. We younger officers were not excited because we had served under several new commanding generals. There was such a great shortage of officers for all ranks that a new general was as common as a new truck or tank.

The morning that Gen. Patton was to assume command I started working without remembering that it was the day Gen. Patton was to arrive. As a first lieutenant, I would not have any military function nor duty assignment for the new commander's arrival. In a few days I would be asked for reports on my area of work.

An hour before Gen. Patton's arrival time, we heard sirens screaming in the distance. The sirens seemed to be coming from the main post area of Fort Benning. The sirens were so loud we were certain that several buildings were burning. Some of our staff officers who had field glasses attempted to locate smoke from the main post area. One officer remarked, "The sirens seem to be coming our way. We must have a fire in our area."

We walked around our building trying to see the location of any fire in our camp. Suddenly a dozen motorcycles roared into our camp with their sirens screaming full blast! Every motorcycle rifleman was wearing a gleaming helmet with the insignia of the 2nd Armored Division, Gen. Patton's Hell-on-Wheels Division. Every man dismounted from his motorcycle and grabbed a polished rifle. They surrounded our buildings with their rifles ready to fire! Not one of the riflemen spoke to us. I am sure that enemy troops would have shown more interest in us! It was half an hour before the time set for Gen. Patton to assume command.

One of our senior officers commented, "We're sure going to be in for something!"

We went inside our headquarters and tried to get back to work, thinking this would be what Gen. Patton would want us to be doing when he arrived. Again we heard sirens in the distance. We could hear the rumble of heavy track-laying vehicles. We had not had rain for several days. The track-laying vehicles were curling up clouds of dust! It had to be Gen. Patton coming!

In advance of Gen. Patton were two light tanks followed by several armored track-laying personnel carriers. These carriers had armor plate for the protection of a dozen armed soldiers. In the convoy with the tanks were two army trucks carrying more soldiers, and we were to discover they carried an American flag, the flag of the I Armored Corps, and the flag of a two-star general. We had only one American flag in our area without any flags in front of our headquarters; no flag for our I Armored Corps and no flag for any general because our Commanding General had already retired. When the convoy stopped in front of our building, the flags were posted in flag stands also furnished by the soldiers from the 2nd Armored Division. The flag posting ceremony was done with sharp commands and heel-clicking precision. All of the flags were covered. Gen. Patton's soldiers formed in a double rank opposite our headquarters building. Five of the soldiers remained with the covered flags. Every soldier was at rigid attention except for the automatic riflemen who were holding their rifles in position ready to fire. I could see their fingers on the triggers and was concerned that they could have live bullets! By the time the ceremony of posting the covered flags in the flag stands was finished, all of the I Armored Corps staff were outside watching. Our Chief of Staff suggested, "Perhaps we should try to get into some sort of military formation."

We lined up opposite the soldiers from Gen. Patton's 2nd Armored Division. There was a contrast in our military procedures and our appearance. Gen. Patton's soldiers lined-up with commands, "Dress right! Dress!" Every soldier clicked into a straight line. We sauntered into a wavy line without any commands. We wore different uniforms! Some of our officers were in winter uniforms, and some were in part summer and part winter uniform. Some of our officers insisted on wearing the insignia and shoulder patch of their old cavalry or field artillery units. Few of us had the insignia of the I Armored Corps. Some wore the overseas cap, the flat type; others wore the cap with the bill, the garrison type; some were without any headgear; one officer wore a campaign hat which was first used in the War with Spain! We whispered and talked with each other. Gen. Patton's men were so silent and stern that we stopped our whispering. A master sergeant shouted, "Attention!" and Gen. Patton's men snapped to attention. We attempted to stand erect because coming into our area was a shiny World War II command car - no top, two seats and a bar on the front seat to give support when riding in a standing position in the back seat. Standing erect at the bar was Gen. Patton! The command car stopped in front of the men from the 2nd Armored Division. Gen. Patton ignored us; not even a glance or smile in our direction. As he dismounted from the command car, one of our officers whispered, "Here comes a tear jerking speech!"

A Commander Will Command

Gen. Patton approached his men, stopped, clicked his heels and saluted. The sergeant was ready with a salute, and when they dropped their hands, Gen. Patton shouted, "Dismissed!"

Gen. Patton continued to ignore us and walked to the front of our headquarters building. The five men standing by the covered flags were at attention.

The General ordered, "Sergeant! Post the Colors!"

Gen. Patton snapped into a salute, and held it as the men uncovered the bright new flags. Gen. Patton dropped his hand salute and ordered, "Dismissed!" He did a left-face, and marched toward us. In front of us he did a rigid right-face. He did not salute us nor speak. The soldiers of the 2nd Armored Division were driving away from our area. The soldiers attempted to hide their sobbing under their shiny helmets.

Gen. Patton looked at his wrist watch. It was a few minutes before eleven; the hour to assume command! I am sure he was counting the seconds until eleven. His eyes did not meet ours. He gazed over our heads into the sky.

Suddenly he saluted us. We returned his salute and he started speaking, "I assume command of the I Armored Corps! At ease!"

With this command we could stop standing at attention and place our hands behind our backs with the left foot moved away from the right, a more restful position. None of our senior officers said, "Welcome." No one moved. Not a word from Gen. Patton, such as, "Glad to be aboard," "Glad to join you!" or "We will make a great team!" Nothing was said as we waited for Gen. Patton to speak again.

Still at attention, Gen. Patton commenced, "We are in a long war against a tough enemy. We must train millions of men to be soldiers! We must make them tough in mind and body, and they must be trained to kill. As officers we will give leadership in becoming tough physically and mentally. Every man in this command will be able to run a mile in fifteen minutes with a full military pack including a rifle!"

One of our over-weight senior officers chuckled.

"Damn it!" Gen. Patton shouted, "I mean every man of this command! Every officer and enlisted man - staff and command; every man will run a mile! We will start running from this point in exactly fifteen minutes! I will lead!"

Gen. Patton stopped speaking but his eyes moved slowly until he caught the eyes of every officer. The silence was so great the sun seemed to stop in the sky. The two stray dogs always running around our area, stopped running and remained motionless as if at attention waiting for Gen. Patton's next command. There was no doubt in the minds of any man, nor in the minds of the two stray dogs, Gen. Patton was in command!

In today's business world and in the military organizations, many executives are commanders only in the title. It is easy to tell the true commanders from the title-only types by listening to conversations. I overheard such a conversation in a military officers' club. It was before noon on the anniversary of the establishment of the United States Air Force. There was to be a big party in the club to celebrate the separation of the Army Air Corps from the Army. I was half asleep in the lounge. I was in almost total darkness watching the Assistant Club Manager arranging glasses and counting the bottles of liquor available for the evening. He did not know that I was in the lounge.

The Club Manager came into the lounge and gave a direct order to the Assistant Manager, "You gotta set up a temporary bar at the back door for tonight!"

"Why?" The Assistant asked.

"Because the General said so!"

The Assistant, "The General also said he wants this club to show a profit. The General cannot have a profit and a temporary bar at the back door!"

"I'm not going to take the heat for not having that bar where the General wants it. When he tells me what he wants, I am going to do what he wants!"

The Assistant continued to count bottles, saying, "No problem. I'll take the heat. I do not mind telling the General he cannot ride two horses going in two different directions. He cannot have a profit and a back-door bar."

"It's only a few hours several hundred people will be here. Can you get a bar tender for a set-up at the back door by evening?"

"Sure!" the Assistant replied, "But do you have any idea of the cost in relation to the number of drinks we would sell at that back door? We would not sell enough to pay for half of the bar-tender's wage. I know from experience."

"The General will be angry! I told him we would have a bar at the back door," the Manager pleaded.

"Tell the General we cannot afford to have his special back-door bar!"

"You think I am crazy! I'm not going to tell him that!"

"Then I'll tell him! I'll call his office after lunch. Stop worrying!"

The Manager pointed his finger at the Assistant, "I want you to know that you have to accept the full responsibility for disobeying the General!"

"No problem! I'm following his orders to put this club on a profitable basis."

A Commander Will Command

"Did I make myself clear that I am not going to take any blame for this?"

"You did! I'll tell the General that four bars are enough for this crowd. We do not need a bar at the back door."

"The General said he did not want any one to wait for a drink," the Manager insisted.

"They can wait a few minutes without a drink as well as with a drink. Stop worrying about the General. I'll show him the profit he wants."

I have reported this conversation from my notes on the exact words. It is quite clear that the Assistant Manager was the true commander. He was in command of the Manager and the General, neither of whom understood the primary mission. In today's business world this conversation is repeated many times every day with little change in titles of the office or in the problem for the command decision. Many executives hold the title of a commander, but some assistant or secretary makes the command decisions.

I had not planned to attend this party, but I could not resist going so that I could enter by the back door to check on the bar! No back-door bar existed! The Assistant Manager remained in command!

When General Patton was in command everyone knew who was in command and who would make the decisions. In addition, Gen. Patton would make sure every soldier knew the primary mission. There was never any doubt in the mind of any soldier about Gen. Patton. Gen. Patton was the Commander!

SUMMER SOLDIERS WILL BE TRANSFERRED
BEFORE THE SUN GOES DOWN

Before Gen. Patton dismissed us from our first meeting, he pulled a bundle of papers from the inside pocket of his blouse. The military term for a coat was "blouse" in World War II. With the papers in his hand, Gen. Patton announced, "I have orders for the transfer of every officer of the I Armored Corps! Every order is signed and dated today. Every officer refusing to run a mile or wanting a transfer will leave this command before the sun goes down!"

Gen. Patton was wearing what I would learn was his war face. He shouted, "Those officers wanting to remain in I Armored Corps under my command will be back at this point in fifteen minutes with full pack ready to run a mile! Dismissed!"

It was a silent I Armored Corps staff that waited to speak until Gen. Patton was inside our headquarters. One senior colonel said, "Gentlemen, it has been great serving with all of you, but I am taking this chance to get out. Anybody want to go with me? I can get good assignments for anyone wanting to transfer to a new armored division being formed at Fort Knox."

The arguments commenced on the advantages and disadvantages of staying and leaving. As the youngest officer, no one asked me to transfer, and no one asked me to stay. From my Carolina experience with Gen. Patton, I could not see anything unreasonable about his demands. I knew I could not run a mile in fifteen minutes with a full military pack. I did not have a full military pack! Most of our staff had only bedding rolls. We did not have enough rifles for all of our guards!

As I waited for the full-pack run, I thought about

Summer Soldiers Will Be Transferred
Before The Sun Goes Down

Gen. Patton's harsh procedure of transferring every officer who wanted out of his command. How unlike the procedures I had learned in college courses on management. So many military and civilian executives assumed command with the words, "It will take me a few months to learn the company policies!" And, "I do not expect to make any changes in the great traditions of this company." Or, "I will try to stay on the same course." All such statements were supposed to unite the members of an organization - unite them in the belief that they could continue the same failing policies of the past. Gen. Patton attacked "summer soldiers" the first minute he was in command.

I rolled my bedding roll and strapped on my empty pistol holster; my full pack! No rifle, no shells, no canteen, almost nothing required to have a full military pack for a soldier. At exactly the time specified, Gen. Patton came to the porch of our headquarters to review his staff. We lost several officers on the quick transfers. Gen. Patton's war face was gone. He was smiling, "I do not see a single rifle on any of you. None of you have a full military pack so we will not run today! But get in shape! You will be doing a mile run every day! Let's meet at the Fort Benning Officers' Club and have lunch!"

A general's desire was a command, so we met at the Officers' Club for lunch. By prearrangement, Gen. Patton had reserved a table for the exact number of the men he knew would be present after the transfers. As I remember we had sixteen officers before the transfers. We had ten officers after the transfers. The moment we were all introduced by our Chief of Staff, Gen. Patton started his attack on the problems of I Armored Corps. He knew more about our organization than we did! He outlined his plans, set time limits on training, and scheduled every day of the week for a month. During the session Gen. Patton did not give any indication that he had ever seen me. He never called me by name; all references were to me as the G-4 which was my duty assignment. I had the answers on the status of our arms and equipment.

Despite my being able to answer all of Gen. Patton's questions, he announced that Col. Hobart Gay would be arriving to assume the duties of G-4. He said that I would be Col. Gay's assistant. With this announcement he did not call me by name; only by rank.

Our lunch continued most of the afternoon. At a break in one of the sessions, one of our senior colonels congratulated me on being assigned as Assistant G-4 for the Corps. Being a civilian reserve officer, I asked, "Is that good? I thought I was being demoted from the position of acting G-4."

"Is that good? You are set for promotions as fast as the days go by! You could never expect to stay on as G-4 as a lieutenant. The job calls for a colonel or one star general. The assistant G-4 calls for a full colonel. You are only a first lieutenant. You will be holding a position four ranks above your present rank. "The colonel was not jealous because he would soon have the star of a general. Although I was not serving in the Army for promotions, I was annoyed that Gen. Patton had not recognized me nor commented on the Carolina maneuvers.

Later in the week the General's Aide told me to be at the General's tent at seven in the evening. At this evening meeting, we refought the battles of Carolina and laughed over the "captured" railroad tank cars. He returned my National Geographic map! He told me about Col. Gay, when he would arrive, and the years Col. Gay and the General had served together.

A few days later, Col. Gay arrived to assume the work of the office of G-4. Col. Gay became Lt. Gen. Gay and was Gen. Patton's Chief of Staff for Third Army during World War II. Col. Gay and I became close friends. It was Gen. Gay who was riding with Gen. Patton when Gen. Patton was injured in the auto accident in Germany.

Before Gen. Patton assumed command of I Armored Corps, we were a group of men shuffling papers, trying to get the men and equipment to fill the assignments of an Armored Corps. The instant Gen. Patton assumed command, we were a team dedicated to one objective; kill the enemy. I thought of Tom Paine's words when Gen. Patton transferred every wavering officer. I am sure Gen. Patton knew the words of Tom Paine: "These are the times that try men's souls. The summer soldier and the sunshine patriot will, in this crisis, shrink from the service of their country . . .."

These were the words Tom Paine had written during the dark days of the Revolutionary War in 1776. Gen. Patton would not have any summer soldiers on his staff.

KEEP A QUICK LINE OF COMMUNICATION

At one our first staff meetings in January, 1942, Gen. Patton announced, "The war in Europe is over for us. England probably will fall early this year. It is going to be a long war. Our first chance to get at the enemy will be in North Africa. We cannot train troops to fight in the desert by training in the swamps of Georgia. I have sent a report to Washington requesting orders moving us to a desert training center in California. The California desert can kill quicker than the enemy! We will lose a lot of men from the heat, but the training will save hundreds of lives when we get into combat. I want every officer and section to start planning on moving all of our troops by rail to California."

In less than sixty days every I Armored Corps unit was a on troop trains enroute to Indio, California. Our final destination was a point in the middle of the desert near the town of Desert Center which in 1942 had a total population of nineteen people! We became two commands, I Armored Corps and the Desert Training Center.

Our headquarters was approximately fifty miles east of Indio, California. Radio reception was poor due to the long distance between our small portable radios and the broadcasting stations in Palm Springs and Los Angeles. Gen. Patton's first concern was always the welfare of the troops so he purchased a radio broadcasting transmitter. The initial investment was with his own money! Our Signal Corps troops installed the radio broadcasting equipment. The station broadcasted only news and music. This radio station gave Gen. Patton a quick way to talk to the troops.

Gen. Patton talked to the troops as often as possible. At a staff meeting, he said, "This· new radio station will save several weeks of training time. We can reach the troops, every one of them, as often as we need. In an emergency we could reach every man in seconds."

Our desert radio broadcasting station had one unusual feature. There was a microphone in Gen. Patton's office and a second microphone was by his bed in his tent. Day and night Gen. Patton could cut off all news or music and announce a special message or order from his personal mike. When the music clicked off we knew we would hear, "This is Gen. Patton!"

Often Gen. Patton would say, "I want every man to be alert tomorrow because we will be doing the maneuvers for a lot of brass from Washington who don't know the first form thing about tanks or desert warfare. We must show them how wars can be won with speed. I am counting on every man!"

The radio would click, and the radio program would return. There was no signing-off by Gen. Patton. He said what he wanted to say and clicked off. He never hesitated in using the radio to remove an officer from command. Often his harsh words to an officer would provoke laughter. For example, one time Gen. Patton ordered, "Col. Blank, you are removed from command immediately. You hear me? If you know what is good for you, you will stay away from me for a week!"

The usual removal-from-command was accompanied with the order to appear before Gen. Patton immediately. There were many different reasons for removing officers from command. Usually it was because of a difference in training and strategy. Many National Guard and Reserve Officers had been trained in only defensive strategy. Gen. Patton did not believe in defending! He was always on the attack. Any officer who started following the strategy of "digging in" or preparing to defend was certain to be removed from command.

Keep a Quick Line Of Communication

Gen. Patton used the radio to commend special efforts by the troops. He would announce, "Found a damn good soldier today!" He would continue giving the name of the man and his organization. When the officers knew they could be removed in an instant with the click of the radio - and the enlisted men knew they could be given special recognition by Gen. Patton - every man gave his best effort every hour of the day.

Every evening Gen. Patton arranged a type of communication that united all soldiers. This "communication" united us with the soldiers of history! Gen. Patton had buglers blow Taps! Every unit down to a company of two hundred men had their own bugler. With over twenty thousand men sleeping on the ground over a thirty mile strip of the desert valley, we had a hundred buglers.

A bugle for communication during the day in a tank outfit was as practical as a feather in a hail storm. No bugler call could be heard above the roar of the tanks and trucks, but in the stillness of the evening, a bugle call would carry for miles. With sound traveling at the rate of eleven hundred feet per second, it was impossible for all of the buglers to play Taps at the same time. It would take over five seconds for the first note of our Headquarter's bugler to reach a bugler a mile away. Thus, with a hundred buglers blowing Taps at different places and times and with the echoes bouncing off the mountains, it was a sound to cause the mind of every man to pause for a moment in prayer.

Those bugle calls made us feel we were a part of an organization which had the power of the armies of all of the centuries. No soldier could go to sleep after the last echo of the bugle call because the desert coyotes were impressed with the sounds and carried on coyote-conversation from every mountain range. The wails of the coyotes continued for a period of time much longer than the bugles.

Gen. Patton "put us to bed" with the pride of knowing that we were a part of a military organization which united all of the forces of Nature, including the coyotes.

I remember Gen. Patton saying one night, "I love the sound of those bugles! It takes me back to my service in the Cavalry when I was an Aide to Gen. Pershing in the war against Mexico."

PUNISHMENT FOR MISTAKES MUST BE IMMEDIATE, OR A DEAD MAN DOES NOT HAVE ANY EGO!

Gen. Patton's principles of discipline did not match modern rules for management. The idea of giving reprimands in a quiet and personal conversation to avoid hurt feelings was not for Gen. Patton.

I remember his words, "When you make a mistake in war, the punishment is death! The trouble is your mistake could cause hundreds of soldiers to die. In war, the enemy does not give a warning before they shoot! That's not the way war works. If the enemy sees you first, he shoots first!"

In our staff meetings Gen. Patton advised instant punishment for every mistake. Often a staff member would go to the defense of a friend and suggest some softer punishment. When some officer with a degree in management would explain the new ideas for leadership, Gen. Patton would explode, "All that 'save the ego' nonsense is not for leadership in war. A dead man does not have any ego! How long after you touch a burning match does it take before you get burned? You get your punishment instantly by touching the match. That is the way Mother Nature works, and that's the way war works. What happens to the tree that does not put down its roots? Such a tree will die for lack of water or blow over with the first strong wind. Every mistake has its own punishment. How long does it take for a garden rake to hit you in the face when you step on the teeth turned toward you? Didn't you ever stub your toe on a rock? How long after your toe hits the rock does it take for you to feel the pain?"

For all of us who had served on the staff for several months it was difficult to keep from laughing when some

Punishment For Mistakes Must Be Immediate, Or A Dead Man Does Not Have Any Ego

new officer would protest Gen. Patton's harsh reprimands. Some of our new staff officers were transferred from Washington. It was fun when the new officer would attempt to explain what he had learned in Washington. Gen. Patton would stare at the protesting officer for a moment as we would grin knowing that a time bomb was about to explode!

Gen. Patton would start slowly, "Colonel, what happens when you touch hot electric wires?"

The officer would answer, "You get shocked."

"Right!" Gen. Patton would proceed as if he were leading a child. "How long after you touch the electric wires until you get this shock?"

"The shock would come instantly!"

"Right again!" Gen. Patton would react as if the Washington officer was displaying outstanding intelligence. "Now that time span from the touch and the shock is exactly what we try to do with our training for war. A mistake in war can cause instant death for hundreds of men! We are training for war, colonel. We cannot delay punishment when the punishment for a mistake is instant death! There is no point in trying to save the ego of a man if the man is dead! War is a killing business!"

The colonel nodded his head in agreement. One day Gen. Patton continued, "Since we have a little time today, let me explain why harsh punishment is so important. In truth, war is the result of an undisciplined society - a society of people that will not face the truth of discipline. War is a discipline for all of us! Let's get this into our heads. Discipline is a law of Nature! Discipline can be delayed, but it can never be avoided. Mother

Punishment For Mistakes Must Be
Immediate, Or
A Dead Man Does Not Have Any Ego

Nature never lets a wrong go unpunished. The punishment may be years later, and punishment which is delayed will be more severe. Take parents and kids. If the parents cannot spank the kids, the punishment will be given later by the school teachers. Could be in school the other kids will spank the kids that need punishment. The bottom was cushioned for spanking. God and Mother Nature never make any mistakes. If these mean kids are not spanked by the teachers in school, they may be put in jail by the police."

Gen. Patton paused as he looked at every one of us - almost to see if we needed "spanking."

"What happens when we get so many mean kids that the police cannot spank the kids? Self-punishment! Self-punishment is the worst type and the most severe. The kid who cannot discipline himself becomes the man who cannot control his eating and drinking - or his use of drugs. What's the punishment? Liver failure, all kinds of heart problems, lung cancer, and many other severe punishments are given by Mother Nature and God. Could be years later."

Several of us were anxious to leave, but there was no leaving when Gen. Patton was in the middle of a "sermon."

"The saddest part about discipline is that war is the result of a bunch of people who are afraid to spank their kids or put criminals in jail. School is a discipline of the mind. First thing you know, unspanked kids will start insulting their parents and teachers, throwing stones at the school, writing on the walls of public buildings. Why not? There is no punishment! In truth the kids are mad that their parents and the school do not discipline them. Next

Punishment For Mistakes Must Be
Immediate, Or
A Dead Man Does Not Have Any Ego

step is these kids refuse to go into the Army even when drafted. They burn the flag! Or run to Canada. They picket and protest and get little punishment. They might even picket Congress!"

Gen. Patton smiled, "You think I am crazy? Some fool leader will give these young kids some crazy patriotic idea, and they will jump at the wave of his hand. This "Heil Hitler" hand waving is a good example!"

Again Gen. Patton paused to let his ideas "soak" into our minds, "We could blame the German people, but we are not free from blame. We bury the discipline of our laws when our leaders break the law without any fear of punishment. Don't always blame the kids. They follow their leaders. Our political leaders and movie stars admit in public to bribery, adultery, bigamy and many major crimes. And the general public approves! Young people follow the examples set by their leaders. Adults are amazed at the violent crimes of the kids as they applaud the violent crimes committed in the movies. Murder is public entertainment in the movies! Can we be amazed when our kids beat up on older citizens?"

This time Gen. Patton gave a wave of his hand indicating that he was sweeping all of us into being responsible for the acts of our children. Gen. Patton reached these conclusions in 1942 in explaining the basic cause of World War II. This was before our society "rocked" into discord music! Gen. Patton continued, "Next thing you know, to get votes, Congressmen will start cutting money for the Army. You have heard the statements from our top leaders, "We do not want war!" What man in his right mind ever wanted war? Certainly not the military! The military have to fight the wars caused by those preaching peace at any price."

"There is no possible way that any of us can avoid the punishment of Mother Nature. A group of young men at a university in England recently said that they would never give their lives for their country. What happens? The Prime Minister of England starts saying, 'We want peace in our time.' What was he really saying? He is saying he is afraid to die. He is afraid to go to war! What's the result? Some tin horn spoiled kid, such as Hitler, thinks he can whip any country where all of the people want peace. What results? War! When did the war start? In the minds of the men who were shouting for peace at any price! Church minsters climb into their pulpits and preach fear of war! What they are saying is they are afraid to die. It is impossible to preach fear and faith at the same time from the same pulpit! Christ said we would always have wars. That is a law of Nature!"

This time Gen. Patton paused for several seconds before finishing with words which I shall never forget.
Gen. Patton closed, saying, "In the United States we never go to war. We invite the enemy to attack!"

Gen. Patton looked at the colonel who had made the protest over the harsh punishment, "Colonel, do you understand that war is the result of a basic law of Nature? Would you try to brush away a tornado with the back of your hand?"

"No, sir! Gen. Patton, I would not!" "Then do not expect me to fail to punish instantly when you make a mistake because in war mistakes can take more lives than a tornado! I cannot kill a man in our combat training, but I can make every man wish to be dead rather than face the wrath of my anger!"

Punishment For Mistakes Must Be
Immediate, Or
A Dead Man Does Not Have Any Ego

There was a long silence as Gen. Patton walked back and forth in front of the room. Every man knew that if a mistake was made Gen. Patton's wrath would strike with the speed of lightning. Many years later Gen. Patton's lecture came to me as I stepped on a carpet switch of our burglar alarm system. My "mistake" was in failing to turn off the system before entering the house. Our alarm was an air horn with a high piercing sound which was set off when I stepped on the carpet switch! I never walk over this area of carpet without thinking of the instant "punishment" of that siren - and Gen. Patton's instant-punishment lectures!

The warden of the San Quentin gave Gen. Patton's lecture in a different way when he was asked if he approved of capital punishment. The warden said, "I approve of capital punishment for all crimes! I would put the man in a room with two doors. I would give every criminal the choice of going through either door. I would advise him that one door would give him instant death from a firing squad the instant he opened the door. The other door would permit him to walk out of jail a free man. No criminal, who was lucky to select the door of freedom, would ever commit another crime because of his fear of facing instant death. Those men thinking of committing a crime would think of the firing squad before they would think of any crime to commit. We delay the punishment for our criminals too long, and the punishment is not enough to keep them from committing the same crime again.

The words of the warden were almost the exact words of Gen. Patton, who said so often, "The longer the punishment is delayed, the more severe the punishment."

41

Punishment For Mistakes Must Be
Immediate, Or
A Dead Man Does Not Have Any Ego

We cannot build jails fast enough to house our criminals. What is the punishment for society? Society pays a high price in the higher number of robberies, murders and rapes - of the people who do not discipline their criminals with instant punishment.

Proof that our society fails in the punishment of our criminals is in the entertainment which we enjoy. The movie, "Going In Style," had the theme that living in jail is better than living as a senior citizen! The newspapers of today report people committing crimes so they can have the "luxury" of going to jail!

Many will protest that no one would commit a crime for the sole reason of getting sent to jail. From my experience as prosecuting attorney for crimes committed in Indiana, I can recall several "down and out" types that asked what was the "least" wrong they could do so they could be sent back to jail.

Proof of more crimes being committed when there is delay of punishment is in the Bible. Thousands of years ago more crimes were committed when "sins were forgiven." From Romans, Chapter 5, verse 20, "Sin will abound when all sins are forgiven by grace."

War is the punishment of a society that fails to face harsh discipline. War can change society as suddenly as a person can change a life style in an instant. Our terrible loss at Pearl Harbor changed our society in less than twenty-four hours from wanting peace to demanding that we go to war. We never had such a "uniting" day for our war in Viet Nam.

I remember December 7th for the change which it made in the lives of two men in two completely different life styles; one in jail and one in a church pulpit.

Punishment For Mistakes Must Be
Immediate, Or
A Dead Man Does Not Have Any Ego

On Monday morning, December 8th, I started the day with my usual routine of going to the jail to arrange for the release of our soldiers arrested over the weekend by the civilian police. One soldier was a heavy drinker and never missed being arrested every Saturday night. It was one way of getting a place to sleep and warm meals for Sunday. Often he would take a taxi to the jail! This man was an unusual soldier in that he had enlisted on New Year's Day in top hat and tails - and drunk from a party the previous night!

I will never forget his face as he watched for me through the bars of the jail. He called to me in a stern voice, "Lieutenant! Get me out of here!"

It was not a plea. It was a command and not his usual Monday morning unsober voice.

When I was closer to him, he said, "Get me out of here, and I will never drink another drop of liquor. I want to do everything I can to fight for our Country!"

You can speak of being reborn, resurrected, or changing a life style. The change of this soldier was in a flash. He stop drinking! He had leadership ability and a driving desire to serve his Country. In less than sixty days he was in OCS (Officer Candidate School) and graduated to become one of our finest officers.

The other man, the minister, I had met a few times in the local jail as he worked with the members of his flock. I was amazed to see this minister out of the robes of the clergy and in the uniform of a soldier with the bars of a Lieutenant and the cross of a Chaplain.

I had to ask bluntly, "What happened, Chaplain?"

He was blunt in confessing, "I feel responsible for so many young men who will have to go to war. The least

43

Punishment For Mistakes Must Be
Immediate, Or
A Dead Man Does Not Have Any Ego

I can do is go with them. I was preaching a sermon on peace the very instant the Japs were bombing Pearl Harbor. Peace will never come by preaching for it."

Later he quoted Gen. Washington many times in chapel services, saying, "The way to peace is to prepare for war."

These two men were not alone in their instant life-change. Neither of these men had been under Gen. Patton to learn of his principles for peace. Tragic as it is, there is truth in the words that Pearl Harbor was necessary to change the thinking of our people.

About forty years after the young men in the club at the university of England had resolved that they would never give their lives for their country, this same club resolved that they would serve their country even at the cost of their lives. They added an additional resolution that their club had to share the blame for the failure to fight Hitler at the beginning of his attack on other nations.

So many times Gen. Patton said, "There is only one kind of discipline, perfect discipline, which gives the punishment at the same instant the mistake is made. When we do not maintain discipline we can cause hundreds to be killed."

War is the delayed punishment for the society that does not believe Christ who said, "There will always be wars and rumors of wars."

Often Gen. Patton used these words and added, "I wish Christ had told us how to avoid war!"

SAY WHAT YOU MEAN
AND MEAN WHAT YOU SAY!

Men cannot be excited to kill with soft words spoken in an uncertain voice. When Gen. Patton spoke, every man knew exactly what was demanded.

Gen. Patton explained, "It takes a lot of talking to get our American young men ready to kill; to murder. Killing is against their nature. The language of war is not polite. War is hell! A hell caused by society for the young men in military service. It is difficult to make a fine American young man understand that the enemy wants to kill him. We have to work hard to keep our men from being killed. We have to work even harder to get them ready to kill the enemy. Swearing helps get the idea across. When I give a command and put in enough profanity, the soldiers will understand. I use the language of combat soldiers. They know what I mean! Another thing, I always wear a war face. There dare not be any smiling when you give orders. War is not a smiling business. I will shoot any one of you who ever has his picture taken with a smile on his face for a news camera!"

When he gave the "war face" lecture, I thought of the Indians who painted their faces for war. Gen. Patton did not miss a trick in preparing the troops for war. With profanity Gen. Patton secured the objective of always getting his message to the soldiers.

There is not much of a command in the words, "By the way, in the morning, weather permitting, we may decide to attack the enemy; I guess, if we all agree."

In time of peace the society of a true democracy often wants a military commander to take a vote of the troops for every command decision. I state with pride that I was awarded a Freedom Foundation award for writing a magazine article stressing that our United States was not a true democracy despite the use of this word by our current public office holders. In the magazine article I quoted the statement of Gen. C. P. Summerall, Sec. of War for President Roosevelt. Gen. Summerall said, "One of the earliest forms of government, and one of the worst, was the true democracy, in which every question was submitted to the will of the people. We see outbursts of this even in our own day (1933) in what is known as mob rule. It (true democracy) naturally and inevitably degenerated into demagoguery."

It is amazing that in America our society sings the Battle Hymn of the Republic and gives the Pledge to the Flag and to the Republic for which it stands, praying for true democracy! Our public office holders take the oath of office "to support and defend our Constitution" which provides for a republican form of government.

It is necessary for candidates for public office to stress "true democracy" if they want to get elected! Our society wants polls taken "on the will of the people" on every decision of government. Poll taking is a form of mob rule! Candidates for office have to use "soft words" to avoid stirring up the mob rule of a peaceful society!

Gen. Patton's commands left nothing to "the will of the soldiers." He would order an attack by saying, "By God, at exactly five in the morning we are going out and kill every damn one of those SOBs!"

It should be mentioned that for many years our federal government had a Secretary of War and a Secretary for the Navy. When these two offices were combined with the Army Air Corps, the Department of Defense was established. I am sure Gen. Patton caused an uproar in Heaven that our Country would let the world know that we would do nothing except defend. He hated the word, defense. He said so many times, "Let the enemy defend! We will always be attacking!" It would be an interesting bit of research to decide if we have had more troubles with foreign nations since we let them know we do not have a War Department.

When speaking to a large group of soldiers, Gen. Patton never read his speech nor used any written notes; not even index cards. If a mike was needed, he never touched the long pipe from the ground to the mike, which was adjusted for his tall height. When he threatened punishment his hand would be on one of his pistols.

Many years later I learned from his daughter that he had dyslexia, which made it hard for him to read. His eyes raced in all directions over the words without any regular reading pattern. This would explain his great memory and lack of need for any speech notes. "Reading" over the words so many times the words would "freeze" in his memory. This reading problem is the reason he could quote so many verses of the Bible as I mention later.

Those who heard Gen. Patton's profanity, assumed he was always in a fit of anger. His fits of anger were the methods he used to excite the troops. An angry soldier is more dangerous than a smiling soldier. After Gen. Patton's fit of anger before the troops he would return to a staff meeting and be as calm as a church elder. He would ask whether or not the troops received the message. Some of us always had to be among the troops to get the reaction of the soldiers.

The soldiers who saw Gen. Patton in "profane action" would never suspect that he was acting his role as a leader. On the staff we knew he was trying to act as the great military leaders of history had acted. Gen. Patton

Say what you mean
and mean what you say!

admired Alexander and attempted to imitate his methods of leadership. We knew he was acting because he told us so many times that we should try to imitate great military leaders. In lectures I have mentioned that Gen. Patton acted every day of his military life. I have also said that his timing was better than any modern day speaker. A great actress confirmed my statements.

Lyn Fontanne, the actress and wife of Alfred Lunt, described Gen. Patton's stage ability. Before her death, Lyn Fontanne was interviewed on television. She was asked, "What was your greatest experience on stage?"

She answered immediately, "I was in Paris during the World War II. We had finished our show and taking our curtain calls when some one in the audience shouted, 'Gen. Patton is here!"

The house lights were dim so I could not see the audience. I went to the microphone and asked, "Would Gen. Patton please come on stage, if you are here?"

Before I could finish speaking, the audience raised a deafening cheer with whistles and loud hand-clapping. The cheers continued so I knew he was in the theater. I never saw him as he left the theater because the audience was standing. My first glimpse of him was as he came from the right side of the stage. He was tall, and with his uniform and medals he seemed too tall to come through the door. He was wearing his shiny helmet, which he removed and held over his heart with his left hand. I was sure the roof would fly away as the audience cheers increased when he stepped in full view for the audience. I stepped back to offer the microphone to him. He winked and nodded his head to me. I shall never forget it! He marched half-way towards me, stopped, clicked his heels, did a right-face. clicked his heels again and saluted the audience as he held

48

his helmet. The cheering increased. I was the only one who could hear his heels click He held the salute for the perfect amount of time. When he lowered his hand salute, he did another right face with precision and walked off stage. He did not say a word - never smiled nor gave a polite wave of his hand! As an actor his timing was perfect. His salute was the perfect "speech" to give to such an audience. I am sure that crowd cheered for an hour after he left. Alfred and I did not leave, but I can assure you we did not get to our hotel until a late hour. Beyond any doubt that cheering for Gen. Patton was my greatest experience on any stage!"

Gen. Patton's acting ability generated a mystic faith in people, especially soldiers. He gave people faith in themselves.

I mentioned Lyn Fontanne's experience one time in a lecture. A man came to me afterward to say, "That cheering in Paris did go on for hours. I was there! I was in uniform and was never so proud to be an American soldier! The French would not let us leave! Everyone shook our hands as if some of Gen. Patton's spirit would get through to them from touching us."

There was one time I was not certain whether Gen. Patton was acting or actually in a rage. One night he knocked his turned-on flashlight into one of the holes of our open-pit latrine. We had the GI right-angle flashlights with the belt clip for walking at night. It was easy to knock this flashlight over when it was setting on a table or toilet seat. The pit for our latrine was about six feet deep. The flashlight in the bottom of the latrine continued to glow. It was a most unusual sight to enter the latrine in the middle of the night and see the soft light glowing through our six open seats giving the holes the indirect

Say what you mean
and mean what you say!

lighting usually found in night clubs!

Gen. Patton's anger or acting continued into the morning briefing session of the staff. He said, "I am the idiot that knocked his flashlight into the latrine last night. Put the cost of the flashlight on a charge sheet to me. I do not want such a loss to be charged off as a battle casualty!"

Everyone laughed. Playing with the idea, he continued, "On second thought, I have a couple of commanders I know who are better qualified at digging out that flashlight than they are at leading troops. I may assign them the mission of digging out the latrine!"

No one knew the commanders who were in line for the flashlight mission. Every man who heard the story tried harder to avoid Gen. Patton's assignment of digging out the flashlight.

After the first few days of hearing Gen. Patton swear, his profanity did not seem to be disrespectful of God. When Gen. Patton asked God to damn something, somehow it seemed to us that God would obey! We knew that if God did not listen, there would be no end of trouble! Gen. Patton's relationship with God was as if two old friends were showing their friendship with words of abuse. Gen. Patton was fighting for God!. God should co-operate! His prayer for fair weather for fighting is an example:

"Almighty and most Merciful Father, we humbly beseech Thee to restrain these immoderate rains, grant us fair weather for battle, graciously hearken to us as soldiers who call upon Thee, that armed with Thy Power, we may advance unto victory and establish Thy Justice among men and nations." Gen. Patton expected God to get the message!

This call to God was following the pattern of Alexander who always kept his soldiers aware that he was getting his ideas from Zeus, the Greek God.

Gen. Patton's daughter, Mrs. James W. Totten (Ruth Ellen) reviewed the text for this book and commented about one of her father's prayers: "Another interesting thing that few people notice is the similarity between the prayer of Achilles at the siege of Troy, and the prayer my father put on his Christmas card to the soldiers at the Battle of Bastogne. The Achilles prayer was as follows; "O Father Zeus, save us from this fog and give us a clear sky so that we can use our eyes. Kill us in daylight if you must."

Ruth Ellen continued, "One of the Chaplains asked my father if a Christian should appeal to a heathen God in such a way? Isn't that blasphemous? My father answered, 'Am I less of a man than Achilles who asked his God for help as I pray to mine?' God is God no matter what you choose to call Him."

Often Gen. Patton would stress how to speak when giving orders. He stressed the importance of giving commands in such a way that soldiers would obey. He often said, "I can tell a commander by the way he speaks. He does not have to swear as much as I do, but he has to speak so that no one will refuse to follow his order. Certain words will make you sound like a staff officer and not a commander. A good commander will never express an opinion! A commander knows! No one cares what your opinion is! Never use the words, "In my opinion, I believe, I think, or I guess - and never say I don't think!" Every man who hears you speak must know what you want. You can be wrong but never be in doubt when you speak! Any doubt or fear in your voice and the troops can feel it. Another thing! Never give a command in a sitting position unless you are on a horse or on top of a tank!"

Say what you mean
and mean what you say!

Many writers called Gen. Patton flamboyant without ever understanding why Gen. Patton's angry voice.

I enjoy watching and listening to candidates for public office. It is interesting to watch the candidates who "know" exactly what they are going to do when they get elected. This type of "command" candidate usually will defeat the candidate who says, "Well, I think, or my best advisers tell me." An often cited quote can be used as an example. Few can forget the candidate for President who said, "I talked to my daughter and she said her friends told her . . .." That candidate was defeated!

When Gen. Patton spoke to the troops he did not quote from opinions, advisers, or rely on anyone unless it would be God - and he would swear by God!

Gen. Patton meant everything he said, and he said it in a manner that left no doubt about what he was saying. It was common for some freshman news reporter to ask, "General Patton, may I quote you in my newspaper on what you just said?"

The General would answer in disgust with his meanest war face, "You can quote me anywhere you like on every damn word! If I had not meant what I said, I would not have said it."

ANY MAN WHO THINKS HE IS INDISPENSABLE, AIN'T

Gen. Patton did not use "ain't" in his usual conversation. When he used "ain't" with this principle, the power of the principle struck with greater speed - when seasoned with profanity.

Gen. Patton explained, "In war every man is expendable. That includes me! Any man who thinks he is indispensable already is not worth his weight in anything. I will transfer such an officer immediately. Every man must be willing to give his life to accomplish the mission, but do not lose your life without making several of the enemy lose theirs. Never die alone. Take several of the enemy with you!"

He would continue, "Any man who starts thinking he is indispensable will start staying away from the fighting at the front. He will spend more time in the rear echelons thinking he is too important to risk going where the shells are falling and men are being killed. This man is a coward twice over. He is afraid of himself and of the enemy. In war every man is expendable."

Gen. Patton did transfer officers because of their over-estimation of their importance. I remember one officer who qualified for a transfer in a few seconds. When we were at our base camp in the desert we had a two hour break during the hottest time of the day. Our mail arrived during this extremely hot period. Usually one junior grade officer would walk in the sun to pick up the mail for other staff members. One day a captain announced he was going to the mail room, and a dozen officers asked him to bring back their mail when he returned. The captain never returned with any mail for junior grade officers! Later that evening in the mess tent,

Any Man Who Thinks He is Indispensable,
Ain't

we asked the captain why he never returned with our mail.

The "captain" (now wearing the gold oak leaves of a major), speaking as seriously as a minister announcing a death, said, "Gentlemen, when I picked up my mail I received my letter of promotion to the rank of major. I did not deem it proper for a field grade officer to be carrying mail for junior grade officers."

We were so shocked we could not speak nor laugh! The first notice of a promotion came when the new rank was in front of the name on the envelope enclosing the notice of promotion. In the few seconds when this new major saw his name on the envelope, he became of so little value to the staff that he could not carry mail! It was too crazy to believe.

Just as Gen. Patton advised, "Any man who thinks he is so all-important, already is worthless!" This officer was of no value for the I Armored Corps the instant he received his promotion.

As our I Armored Corps and Desert Training Center grew in troop numbers, our staff became more specialized in duties. Every officer had a specific duty and the proper amount of authority to get the job done. In addition we were supposed to know about the activities of all of the other staff sections. This sharing of information was the reason for our frequent staff meetings.

Gen. Patton advised, "We can expect that some of us will be killed. We do not want the loss of one man to stop our killing the enemy. Always have a man trained and ready to take over your job in case you are killed. The test of your ability is whether you can be killed and nothing would be lost!"

We laughed, but Gen. Patton didn't smile. This principle is not often followed in civilian life. Many

Any Man Who Thinks He is Indispensable, Ain't

corporate executives all the way down to the janitors strive to prove their worth by trying to be indispensable. In civilian life it is called, "empire building." It is a type of job security to keep others from knowing anything about the work done by you or in your section.

Every man was "expendable!" Gen. Patton did not spare himself. He repeated so often, "I do not know of a better way to die than to be facing the enemy when you are shot. When I am facing forward I can keep firing my pistols. Always fall forward! Never fall backwards!"

When I heard Gen. Patton make these remarks about how he wanted to die going forward in combat, I was sure that he was building courage for the men. When I knew him better I was sure that he fully intended to ignore all risks with the hope of being killed leading his troops into combat.

When he said, "Every man is indispensable - including me!" He meant every word.

THE MISSION IS ALL IMPORTANT
THINK ABOUT STANDARD RULES LATER

One afternoon Gen. Marshall was inspecting our Desert Training Command. Gen. Marshall was the Chief of Staff for all of our military units. At this time in the summer of 1941, we were losing the war in North Africa. President Roosevelt and Churchill wanted our troops sent to North Africa. We had so many visiting officers from the Pentagon, we doubted that there were any left in Washington! We were on a small hill or observation point that we called, "Patton's Nose." That is, we called it, "Patton's Nose" when we knew he could not hear us. He knew we called it his nose. In humor, he called this little hill, "The Head! A good place for Pentagon officers!" The Navy called their latrine, "the head."

Through field glasses we were watching the movement of the tanks several miles away. From the little hill we could see for over seventy miles in the flat desert. We had erected two large wall tents with sides rolled up to provide shade for the high ranking officers from Washington. Mrs. Marshall was with her husband. Mrs. Patton was with Mrs. Marshall. This is the only time we ever saw Mrs. Patton in the desert.

The Signal Corps had installed a public address system on the hill and had connected the public address system into the radio network of the tank commanders. The many commands and conversations of the commanders could be heard on the public address system. As we listened to the many officers talking, we could see the dust swirl into the desert where the tanks were racing. Gen. Patton would cut off the commanders radio and explain to the visiting officers the strategy of the attack. Gen. Patton spoke from a mike that was outside of the tent and not

GEN. PATTON'S WAR FACE

GEN. PATTON, THE CHEER LEADER

GEN. PATTON LECTURING TO THE TROOPS

EVERY SOLDIER KNEW HIS MISSION

NEW 1941 LIGHT TANK

LIGHT TANK CROSSING A STREAM

LIEUTENANT GENERAL HOBART GAY
GEN. PATTON'S THIRD ARMY CHIEF OF STAFF

GEN. PATTON IN A MEDIUM TANK

shaded from the sun! He would never in the world stand in the shade as his men worked in the hot sun!

Gen. Patton announced, "Now that the blue army has located the red enemy, the light tanks will go around the right flank and destroy the red enemy from the rear. Our strategy is 'Grab'em by the nose and kick'em in the pants!' Soldiers understand this strategy!"

There were questions from the visiting officers and discussions about the speed of tanks in soft sand. Time elapsed and no light tanks moved to attack the right flank of the red enemy. The desert settled into total calm. The wind blew the swirling dust into oblivion. Nothing was moving except Gen. Patton's anger. Being near him, I could hear him call on one radio channel and then on another trying to reach the light tank commander. All of this was not over the public address system!

Suddenly Gen. Patton announced to the visiting officers, "We have had a mix-up in command. This is exactly how battles are lost in war. The failure to pursue an enemy can cause many men to die. This maneuver is called off until tomorrow morning. I can assure every one of you that this mix-up in command will not happen tomorrow!"

Gen. Patton ordered all of his staff to gather around him below the little hill, the observation point. At this meeting he ordered us to round-up the tank commanders for an immediate meeting at our headquarters a few miles away.

At this meeting with the commanders, Gen. Patton related the battle plans. He explained the failures that could be caused by not making a rapid pursuit of the enemy. The primary failure was pin-pointed on the commander of the light tanks, a young lieutenant. After a short discussion, Gen. Patton called the young lieutenant to the front of the staff meeting.

"Lieutenant, you know the need for speed and fast action. You were in command of the light tank force. Where were you? Why didn't you attack? What radio channel were you using? Why couldn't I reach you on the radio? Why did you fail to answer when I called?" Gen. Patton was trying to be calm. "We are interested in your explanation, Lieutenant!"

The young lieutenant was nervous, but he spoke with conviction, "General, I am under the command of Col. Blank. I knew I was supposed to attack, and we were ready. We were on a radio channel which Col. Blank ordered us to use so that our commands would be secret - so the enemy could not hear. Col. Blank told me never to move out until he gave the orders. I never received the order to attack."

Gen. Patton asked, "What's your explanation, Col. Blank?"

"My radio went dead, General!"

"Then you should have dashed over there on your own two damn feet if nothing else! Radios will always be going dead! We must be ready for such radio break-downs. Colonel, you should have been near enough to the front that you could have thrown a stone on the lieutenant's tank!"

Gen. Patton slapped his leg with his cavalry riding stick which he frequently used as a black-board pointer. He looked out into the desert. I knew he was trying to cool his anger.

"Col. Blank, I want to see you in my office immediately!"

Gen. Patton walked back and forth in front of the

staff with a couple of slaps of his stick on the side of his leg. It was so silent that the slapping of his boot sounded like the explosion of a firecracker. The young lieutenant was standing at rigid attention in front of the high ranking officers.

Gen. Patton put his arm around the lieutenant, saying, "At ease, Lieutenant! What you did was exactly right according to Army Regulations. But let me tell you something, if you want to be a Napoleon, always think of the mission first! Forget about Army Regulations. Army Regulations are written by those who have never been in battle. They write about what they have been told by others. We have only one mission in combat and that is to win! If we do not win, you can forget everything because you will probably be dead. After the battles the officers in the Pentagon can write about what we did wrong!"

So often I remember Gen. Patton advising, "Tell the American soldier what has to be done, and he will do it. Battles are won by determined soldiers who do not spend a split second trying to remember what Army Regulations had to say about what to do when the bullets start flying!"

ALWAYS BE ALERT TO
THE SOURCE OF TROUBLE

Gen. Patton was constantly checking with the troops to make sure they understood every mission. He spent every day and many nights training the troops. I was riding with him one evening at dusk when we were outside our diamond shaped defense. In desert combat there is no front combat area nor rear area for supplies and medical tents. A desert command is the same as a battle ship sailing on the ocean. The guns of a battleship cannot be turned to fire into the battleship, but the guns of our tanks could be turned to fire into our own troops.

With darkness, noise, and the confusion of firing, the troops could get excited and forget the location of our own headquarters which was the center of the diamond shaped area. We chained the guns on the tanks to fire in only one direction, and we used aiming stakes; nothing worked. Any morning after a scare from an enemy attack at night, the guns of our tanks could be aimed directly at the center of our camp. We wanted to prevent the slaughter of our own troops when we reached actual combat and used live shells.

Gen. Patton and I were driving in what would have been enemy territory if we had been in actual combat. As we were driving towards our camp we saw one of the outer guards; a soldier with an automatic rifle. Gen. Patton asked me to approach the guard to make sure he knew his exact duty assignment.

I walked towards the guard who stopped me with the order of "Halt!" His rifle was aimed at me. I gave the correct password, and he told me I could advance as he lowered his rifle. I asked the guard what his duties were. He gave a correct report on his duty assignments.

Always Be Alert To
The Source of Trouble

I continued, "From which direction do you expect trouble?"

The guard pointed to the center of our camp!

I started to discipline him, "That is the center of our camp. The enemy would be in the opposite direction. You pointed to where your buddies would be sleeping!"

He put me in my place, "You didn't ask anything about the enemy. I know where the enemy is! You asked where I expected trouble. I expect trouble from right back there! That's Gen. Patton's Headquarters! That's where I expect trouble!"

I could hear Gen. Patton laughing. He called to me, "Come on back, Williamson. That man understands his mission!"

The guard asked of me, "Who was that?"

I answered, "That was Gen. Patton."

"My God!" the guard exclaimed. "You gotta expect Gen. Patton from all directions!"

Gen. Patton was still chuckling when I climbed into the open command car. He commented, "We are doing better! We are up to the level of the Roman Legions!" Since I did not know anything about the training of the Roman Legions I did not say anything.

Many years later I was reading Gibbon's book, The Decline and Fall of the Roman Empire. I thought of Gen. Patton's words when I read, "It was an inflexible maxim of Roman discipline, that a good soldier should dread his officers far more than the enemy."

SELECT LEADERS FOR ACCOMPLISHMENT
AND NOT FOR AFFECTION

Any officer who flattered Gen. Patton took a great chance of being transferred. Gen. Patton demanded obedience, but not blindness. He never objected to any one opposing his plans if there was a good basis for the altered plan.

I remember Gen. Patton telling his methods of selecting leaders. He said, "Does not make any difference what the rank is for promotion. Could be for a colonel or corporal. Picking the right leader is the most important task of every commander. When I have a promotion to make, I line up all of the candidates and give them a problem I want them to solve. I say, "Men, I want a trench dug behind a warehouse. Make this trench eight feet long, three feet wide, and six inches deep." That's all I tell them. I use some warehouse that has windows or a large knot hole.

While the candidates are checking out the tools they want to use, I get inside the building and watch through the window or knot hole. The men will drop all of the spades and picks on the ground behind the warehouse as I watch. After resting for several minutes, they will start talking about why I want such a shallow trench. They will argue that six inches is not deep enough for a gun emplacement. Others will argue that such a trench should be dug with power equipment. Others will say it is too hot or too cold to dig. If the men are officers there will be complaints that they should not be doing such lowly labor as digging a trench. Finally, one man will give an order to the others, 'Let's get this trench dug and get out of here. Doesn't make any difference what that old SOB wants to do with the trench."

Select Leaders For Accomplishment
And Not for Affection

Gen. Patton would pause before explaining, "That man gets the promotion. Never pick a man because he slobbers all over you with kind words. Too many commanders pick dummies to serve on their staff. Such dummies don't know how to do anything except say, 'Yes.' Such men are not leaders. Any man who picks a dummy cannot be a leader. Pick the man that can get the job done!"

I remember Gen. Patton saying so often, "Do I care whether the men like me! We are fighting a war! We can be killed, and should be, if we do not pick good leaders! War is a killing business. We have to teach the troops how to save their lives and kill the enemy. You must pick men who can get the job done! When you are leading you are not in a contest to see how happy you can keep the troops. You are not running for public office."

Gen. Patton did not get angry at officers or enlisted men swearing at him - if they had a good reason. I do not remember any officer calling Gen. a Patton a SOB in his presence. I do remember a captain calling Gen. Patton a damn fool and remaining alive! I should explain that for Gen. Patton there were two types of sons-of-bitches. When he called me a son-of-a-bitch for moving his gasoline by rail, I was not exactly happy, but I could tell he was not angry. If Gen. Patton used the term and smiled, it was a compliment. If he scowled with his war face when he used the term, it was bad news. Gen. Patton seemed to enjoy being called a damn fool when he would try something the troops thought could not be done.

I remember a young Captain, a company commander, who called Gen. Patton a damn fool - not once but several times. Gen. Patton came upon the Captain with all of his men working to dig and winch several of their trucks and tanks back to the solid bank of a stream. There was much shouting and swearing as the men had to wade in sand and mud to inch the vehicles back to solid ground. The Captain was in command and was not to be bothered; not even with Gen. Patton.

Gen. Patton went into a rage, "Captain, I've told you a dozen times to hit that stuff with speed! You can never cross anything trying to creep through sand. The faster you go the quicker you will get through."

The Captain replied with anger equal to Gen. Patton's, "That's exactly the reason I have five vehicles in sand up to the axle, General. Any one trying to cross that stream bed at any speed is a damn fool!"

Gen. Patton scanned the stream bed which was about as wide as the distance from home plate to second base. There was no water in the stream which was as level as a floor except for the five vehicles the Captain was trying to pull out. Gen. Patton walked onto the wet sand and stamped his foot. At the edge of the stream the sand was solid.

"I'll show you how to get a jeep through this stuff. It takes speed!" Gen. Patton took the place of his driver in the jeep.

The Captain stood in front of the jeep. "General, believe me! In the center of the stream everything will sink - even a duck couldn't cross! You'll be thrown out of the jeep like a sack of jelly beans!"

"Give me room! I am going through," Gen. Patton ordered as he backed the jeep up fifty feet before charging the flat sand bed. For half of the distance Gen. Patton skimmed on the wet sand until the jeep suddenly sank deeper than any of the Captain's vehicles. Gen. Patton would have been thrown head first into the sand and mud if the windshield had not been in the upright position.

The Captain called, "Stay where you are, General! I'll send a couple of men to carry you out!"

Gen. Patton shouted back, "Keep your men where they are! If I'm damn fool enough to get in here, I sure as hell am not going to be damn fool enough to let some soldier carry me out. I'm not a casualty yet!"

Gen. Patton sludged through the mud which was halfway to his knees. The work on the other vehicles stopped as everyone watched. Everyone was smiling and holding back laughter.

Gen. Patton walked up the bank and saluted the Captain, "You are right! I am a damn fool. I am going to write an order so no one else will be as big a damn fool. There will be no crossing of anything until some soldier is positive the ground can take the weight of a vehicle. If I had walked to the middle of the stream I would have found that wet spot. We have to know what we are doing if we want to save the lives of our men and vehicles."

Gen. Patton put his arm around the Captain, saying, "You are one fine son-of-a-bitch." Gen. Patton was laughing. All of the soldiers broke into laughter followed by a cheer!

Gen. Patton waved his hand to the troops. "Now don't expect me to entertain you for the rest of the afternoon. Let's get these vehicles out of the mud; including my jeep!"

EVERY LEADER MUST HAVE AUTHORITY
TO MATCH HIS RESPONSIBILITY

"If you run into any problems, tell them I sent you. You are acting for me! Right or wrong, I'll back you up. But you better be right!"

Gen. Patton used these words in sending staff members to Washington and to other commands. He demanded loyalty from his staff, and he gave total support to every one of us. We knew he would "back us up" although we made a mistake. This back-up support caused every one of us to exert every effort to be right in what we did.

This principle is a basic principle of management which is said in many different ways. One way of saying it, "Never send a boy to do a man's job." The job may require the authority of a man, but some commanders would give staff members the authority of a boy.

Another way of stating this principle is in the Articles of War that no soldier dares question the authority of an officer. This idea is not accepted by some who believe in equal rights, discrimination, and that every one must be treated the same. Such ideas are for peace-time thinking. In war there is no time to question the authority of an officer.

This principle has been a rule of command for centuries. If soldiers could "poll the ranks" to see whether to obey their officers, many lives would be lost. Taking polls is a type of mob rule. The mob (troops), dare not rule in war.

There are three grades of rank in most armies; officers, non-commissioned officers, and enlisted men. By different names these ranks have been used for hundreds of years. There must not be too much "friendship" between these ranks or the authority of the officer is lost. The military term for this is "fraternization."

Gen. Patton told the story of one of his experiences in World War I. "It was a cold night in France. I asked this soldier standing guard outside my tent to come inside for a drink and to get warm around my pot-bellied stove. I knew it was against regulations to fraternize with the troops, but I knew the man was freezing. We had a short drink, and the guard stepped outside. I curled up in my bedding roll after putting on more clothes.

A few weeks later I had a meeting in my headquarters tent with some British and French officers interested in tanks. Right in the middle of our conference, the same guard I had befriended, stepped inside the tent, saying, "Major! Let's you and me have a little drink!"

We laughed as Gen. Patton continued, "Soldiers must be trained to obey their officers. There dare not be any delay in following a command or many lives will be lost. Soldiers get scared. Commissioned officers dare not get scared at any time! Soldiers must be trained to attack enemy positions with never a falter in their attack. Fear of death will scare some, but a true soldier can give his life without any hesitation. Officers have the "commission" to destroy the enemy. The rank on an officer's shoulder gives the authority to make the decisions so necessary in war; that is, if we are to win. And we are going to win!"

Our society is going through the "stages" of equal rights for all and no discrimination among any. This thinking results in mob rule; let everybody decide everything! It is assumed that this thinking is supported by our leaders of management and labor who meet to solve their problems. Much of this thinking is pushed by those favoring the Japanese system of management which tends to let every worker help make policy decisions.

Many of the media assume that the Japanese system and Gen. Patton's principles are completely different. This is completely wrong. As I understand the Japanese management system, it is general policy that every leader must "talk with the troops." This principle was basic with Gen. Patton. He was always talking with the troops to let them know what was happening in the war and what needed to be done. Such "talking" was not one way. Gen. Patton learned of all of the gripes and complaints of the troops, but Gen. Patton made all of the command decisions without any concern over whether the troops would agree.

An example of the Japanese system of management happened during a long-distance telephone interview I was having with a reporter from a large American daily newspaper. This newspaper reporter was stressing the need for management to permit all workers to have a part in making policy decisions for the newspaper. I was stressing that some one person had to have the "command" of the newspaper. I was not winning any points with this reporter who stressed that every worker would work harder if he had a part in the decision- making process.

I won the argument when the reporter broke in, "This interview is ended!" His profanity was almost equal to that of Gen. Patton's.

I assumed he was angry with me so I added, "Sorry! I had hoped we could differ without anger over something... ."

He broke in again, "It is not your fault! Some damned idiot in the computer room decided to make a chip change! He has knocked out all of our computer terminals without letting me know what he was doing! He killed my word processor!"

Every Leader Must Have Authority
To Match His Responsibility

I could not resist saying, "Now you have the answer as to what can happen when the troops can make command decisions."

"You win! I see what you were trying to tell me about Gen. Patton's principle on authority and responsibility. That idiot in the computer room should not have any authority. And he is totally without any responsibility or brains in doing what he did without letting anyone know. I think I'll go down and shoot him!"

"You are making sounds like Gen. Patton!" I teased the reporter.

He laughed, "Gen. Patton was right!" A few times in my military experience I had to give orders to save lives, - not in combat with a shooting enemy but with crippled aircraft. In 1944 I was asked to give a B-26 twin-engine bomber a test flight to check out newly installed radar equipment. On board were a dozen electronic engineers anxious to test their new equipment. Soon after takeoff the right engine started to lose power. The temperature of the engine was increasing as the oil pressure decreased. It was easy to figure out that the engine was getting hot because it was not getting oil. We were less than a hundred feet above the ground when I made the decision to "feather the prop" on the bad engine to prevent burning up the engine.

Feathering-the-prop means the thin edge of the prop is pointed forward. This prevents the flat side of the props from acting as a brake in slowing down the speed of the plane. When the propeller was "feathered," I cut off all of the electrical power to the engineers' radar equipment. When their radar scopes turned black and they saw the feathered prop, the engineers started strapping on their parachutes, getting ready to jump. I shouted above the

69

noise of the over-worked remaining engine, "Any one who jumps at this altitude will be killed!"

There was a door in the belly of the plane the engineers could use to jump. I could not physically keep any engineer from jumping. I shouted again, "If it is necessary to jump, I'll tell you when! We have one good engine. We are not in danger of crashing."

This quieted the engineers except for one who went berserk in his fright. I ordered, "Tie that man up before he jumps out! He'll kill himself." Several of the engineers overpowered their friend. Since they did not have any rope, two of them sat on him to keep him from jumping.

Landing with only one engine was not difficult. As I circled the field preparing to land I thought about Gen. Patton and his principles of rank. Someone had to give the command not to jump or all of the engineers would have jumped out at less than five hundred feet - the lowest altitude to jump to expect the parachute to open with time to slow the fall.

I gave the command and the engineers, acting as non-commissioned officers, carried out the command to keep the one engineer from jumping - this man was the scared soldier who had to obey or he would have been killed. The engineers had followed the time-worn principles of command.

In less than fifteen minutes I made a routine landing on the paved runway. I insisted that this "scared soldier" be taken to the hospital. He was still shaking after he was on the ground. It was not difficult to have my hospital order carried out. I had called the airport control tower to let the control tower operators know we were having engine trouble. The tower operator ordered a fire truck and ambulance to wait for our possible crash landing. The medics (non-commissioned officers) carried out the order to take the scared engineer to the hospital. I was told it took several hours to calm the shaking engineer.

Army Regulations state that there must be complete separation between officers and the troops. This included separate quarters, dining rooms (mess halls) and rest rooms. Officers had the same fears as the soldiers, but the soldiers should not get so well acquainted (fraternized) with the officers to learn that officers were not free from fear.

One time I was "scared" in an odd way in World War II. I was flying from Los Angeles to Florida. I landed to refuel at a small military airport in Texas. I was using the standing urinal in the rest room when a fellow officer came into the rest room. This fellow officer was a young attractive member of the WASP - Womens' Auxiliary Service Pilots. Women, as Service Pilots, were officers! We had only the two ranks for rest rooms; officers and enlisted men. After a long flight in the air, this young lady did not have time to wait nor check on who was in the "Officers" rest room! She had a "command" to go and took the one rest room available; according to her rank!

The authority of military officers is so great in combat that an officer in every command is given the authority to use the 45 cal. hand gun to shoot any enlisted man who turns away from the enemy. This is not common knowledge with the general public who would think such action too drastic. The public decided that Gen. Patton should not have slapped the enlisted man in the hospital although it was obvious the man had deserted from his outfit.

An interesting feature of this face-slap incident was the doctor's report that this man had a high fever. The

Every Leader Must Have Authority
To Match His Responsibility

high fever was not detected until two days after the man had been "protected from his fear" in the hospital. When I read of the two-day delay in the high fever report, I recalled the GI soap trick so many men used to get a trip to the hospital or as a method to get home sooner. A sliver of GI soap, either the green or the yellow type, was used as a suppository. This soap was so strong that it would generate a high fever - usually after two days!

It was impossible to keep men from using the soap to avoid unpleasant duty, but the doctors could "solve" the illness by doing nothing other than keeping the man away from the GI soap! When I read of the two-day delay in the high fever, I puzzled over whether some other patient or a doctor had suggested the soap-suppository trick to "build" a medical record - to get home sooner.

Gen. Patton was given an award in World War I for threatening to shoot any man who turned away from the front. President Truman, in World War I, gave the same command when his men were retreating. Capt. Truman shouted, "Any SOB who isn't back in position in ten seconds will be shot!" After Capt. Truman's command, that battle became a joke in his organization as, "The Battle of Who-Run!" Among soldiers the authority of officers is well known. Every Article of War is read to every soldier early in basic training.

Recently a Navy Lieutenant was quoted as saying, "I was about ready to draw my pistol and shoot any man who failed to help get the damage under control." The Lieutenant's ship had been hit in one of our mini-wars - if there is such a thing as a mini-war.

All of us suffer when our local police do not have the authority to match the responsibility of stopping crime. Our present society wants our policemen shot before they

Every Leader Must Have Authority
To Match His Responsibility

can shoot at the criminal. Our firemen do not have enough authority to put out fires when some of the public block roads and damage fire fighting equipment. We can be sure there would be some changes in police work and fire fighting if we gave these officers the authority of a military officer! When the criminal has more rights (authority) than our police, we can expect to have more criminals.

PROTECT THE TROOPS FIRST!
THE WISHES OF SUPERIOR OFFICERS
ARE SECONDARY

This Patton Principle is the opposite of the usual rule, "Obey all orders no matter what." It does not match the military rule of "Ours is not to reason why, ours is to do or die."

This Patton principle also violates some of Gen. Patton's principles of loyalty. But no officer ever suffered Gen. Patton's anger if a valid reason existed for differing with the General. I know! I differed with him many times but never without reasons. He demanded absolute loyalty when time would not permit discussion.

We had not been in our desert training center a month when Gen. Marshall wanted to move all of our troops to North Africa to engage in combat with the Germans. We were not ready. Gen. Patton worked at the training. I remember his shouting at the truck and tank drivers, "I will shoot any man driving his tank within a hundred yards of another tank!" Get in the habit of staying apart! Make the enemy waste his ammo on only one tank! Never let the enemy get two sitting ducks with one round of fire! Make the enemy make a separate attack on every tank and truck. We will all live longer!"

Every day Patton would rage at the troops to take more caution in preparing for combat. Every night we posted guards as if we were in combat, but we were not ready for combat with any enemy when we could not combat the heat of the desert.

We were in the middle of a morning staff meeting when Gen. Marshall called from Washington. Gen. Patton took the call in front of the staff. We could hear Gen. Patton's side of the conversation, "It takes at least six

Protect the Troops First!
The Wishes of Superior Officers
Are Secondary

weeks to get a man ready to fight in the desert. Anything short of six weeks, and we will lose more men from heat than from the enemy. George, we must give these men more training!" Gen. Patton's argument was stressed with choice words of profanity.

Gen. Patton won the argument over his old friend, Gen. George Marshall, the Chief of Staff for all of our Armies. Gen. Patton and Gen. Marshall were good friends, but friends or not, to swear at the Chief of Staff could be the death of a military career. Gen. Patton never placed his military career above his concern for the troops. Gen. Marshall was being pushed by Churchill to send troops to North Africa to help the British.

Gen. Patton did not know and would not accept any half-way measures. No soldier could be "half-way" ready to kill the enemy. He wanted the troops fully trained physically and mentally to kill. I remember his words, "We are going to move and move fast! We are not going to dig any fox holes and wait for the enemy to come shootin' at us. We will be shootin' at them first! When every soldier can move a mile in fifteen minutes, we will confuse the hell out of the enemy. We will be where the enemy never expect us to be!" Gen. Patton caused Gen. Marshall to slow down the movement of the troops. Gen. Patton raged, "It's a damn waste of the most wonderful manhood of America to send green troops into combat before they are ready. We must train to win!"

As usual, Gen. Patton was right, but he was alone in his thinking. The history of World War II has many examples of failure to always be ready for combat. The result is the loss of many of "the most wonderful manhood of America."

Protect the Troops First!
The Wishes of Superior Officers
Are Secondary

The history of the world would be different if the Pearl Harbor Commanding Generals had followed Gen. Patton's principle of "always protect the troops first!"

Prior to December 7, 1941, many people knew the Japanese naval force was in the Pacific heading towards Pearl Harbor. Our intelligence units had broken the Japanese codes. Our intelligence had intercepted radio conversations from the ships and planes planning the attack on Pearl Harbor. According to reliable reports, they knew the date and the hour of the attack!

All of this information was relayed to Washington. However, President Roosevelt and Gen. Marshall could not believe the Japs would break the international laws of "no killing" without a declaration of war. Roosevelt and Marshall had sound reasons for their thinking. The Japanese representatives were in Washington to negotiate peace. This Jap negotiator said, "It is impossible to negotiate peace when all of your ships and planes are armed and ready to fire. I saw the weapons of war when I landed in Hawaii. If you want to talk peace, we must disarm!" But the Japs did not disarm!

President Roosevelt asked Gen. Marshall to order the Pearl Harbor military to "step down their defenses." The orders were, "Remove the ammunition from the guns. Take a long weekend! We are going to have peace through negotiation!" The war of words would be fought before the war of guns!

Thousands of lives would have been saved in World War II if the "troops had been protected first." Gen. Patton would never obey any order from the President or any Chief of Staff that would unduly endanger the lives of the troops. Gen. Patton would have followed the wisdom

Protect the Troops First!
The Wishes of Superior Officers
Are Secondary

of Gen. Washington, "The way to peace is to be prepared for war."

If Gen. Patton had been in command at Pearl Harbor, he would have "obeyed" the orders from Washington by "scattering the troops" away from any central bombing area. Gen. Patton would have lectured to his commanders, "There is a large enemy task force approaching our area! We have orders from Washington to disarm, but the orders do not say when to disarm!" He would take one of his long silent periods before saying, "We will disarm ten days after that Jap task force is out of our area!. Stay alert! Always be ready for any attack!"

AN ACTIVE MIND CANNOT EXIST
IN AN INACTIVE BODY

"Wars are won by men with strong wills to win and with strong bodies!" Gen. Patton preached.

"A strong will to win is more important than a strong body! Napoleon said, "It takes the sword and the spirit to win in war. The spirit is most important." Men have won battles when totally exhausted and near death from injuries. However, that will to win did not get into the brain without having a strong body. You have to keep the body active to keep all of the juices running to the right places." Gen. Patton never stopped preaching physical fitness.

His death proved that he was right about getting the body "juices" to the right place. The true cause of his death was his being unable to keep his body active. Gen. Patton never wanted to die in bed. After the auto accident, he could not move because of a broken back. The "juices" piled up in his lungs.

In the winter of 1941, we were stationed at Ft. Benning, Georgia. We were the I Armored Corps, the first corps of tanks in World War II. The term, corps, meant that we should have two or more tank divisions in our command. A tank division had approximately fifteen thousand men and approximately seventy tanks of light and medium size. We had never seen a medium tank! We had pictures! Everything we did was based on guesswork and on Gen. Patton's memory of his experiences with tanks in World War I. We did not have any guide on how many men or tanks would be needed to make up a corps. We did have trucks and cars. Most of our equipment matched the trucks and cars of the civilian models on the highway. We were the I Armored Corps in name, but we were short

An Active Mind Cannot Exist
In An Inactive Body

fifty thousand men and all of the fighting equipment for war. I Armored Corps was made up of our staff of fifteen officers plus our Headquarters Company of approximately two hundred men! All of our "big guns" were six inch stove pipes mounted on trucks!

After Pearl Harbor our primary task was to write reports on exactly how many men and how many tanks should be in an armored corps. Every day we sent reports to Washington suggesting what we decided would be needed in men and tanks for a corps. We were in war, but we were working on the paper work to prepare the proper tables of organization and the tables of basic allowances for a corps of tanks. The terms used were; "TO" for Table of Organization and "TBA" for the Table of Basic Allowances for the equipment.

Every day we received new TO's and TBA's from Washington. We had to study these charts and propose changes when we did not approve. Our approval was based on our experiences with the men and equipment in the field under combat conditions or as near combat conditions as Gen. Patton could create! For our combat conditions we used four door sedans for tanks and stove pipes for our guns mounted on trucks. The war was raging in Europe and in the Pacific, but we were "firing" stove-pipe guns and "shooting" paper reports to Washington.

This type of work did not require any physical exertion. We had office desks and office chairs to sit in as we puzzled over our paper work. Gen. Patton "provided" the exercise! He demanded that every man run a mile every day. This was thirty years before jogging became the thing to do.

Frequently Gen. Patton would stop at my desk and

An Active Mind Cannot Exist
In An Inactive Body

ask, "How long you been sitting at that desk? Get up and get out of here! Your brain stops working after you sit in a swivel chair for twenty minutes. Keep your body moving around so the juices will run to the right places. It'll be good for the brain! If you sit in that chair too long all of your brain power will be in your shoes. You cannot keep your mind active when your body is inactive!"

Every hour of the day was filled with work and physical exercise! Gen. Patton kept our bodies and our minds active!

MAKE THE MIND CONTROL THE BODY
NEVER LET THE BODY COMMAND THE MIND

I remember Gen. Patton saying, "Now if you are going to win any battle you have to do one thing. You have to make the mind run the body. Never let the body tell the mind what to do. The body is always ready to give up and quit. It is always tired; morning, noon and night. The body is not tired if the mind is not tired. When you were young the mind could make you dance all night, and the body was never tired. You could go home from work and be dead-tired until some girl would call asking you to dance! Suddenly the mind assumed command and told the dead-tired body that it was not tired! You had ten times more energy to dance than you had when you went to work in the morning. It is the same way in war. When you are tired, the enemy is tireder! You always have to make the mind take over and keep the body going. Never let the body command the mind. No matter how tired we are, we will never let the enemy rest. We will rest after we have destroyed the bastards!"

The mind can control the body. It is common for us to decide what our bodies cannot do before the body ever gets a chance to try. I am a leg amputee. My mind decided all of the many tasks of work which I could not do on one leg.

One day I saw a man with no legs using crutches on a sandy beach - with no legs touching the ground! That double amputee taught me to try everything. My mind had decided that I could not climb a ladder on one leg and two crutches until I saw a dog go bounding up a ladder. A dog does not have any hands to hold a ladder! A dog's legs on a ladder are about the same as four crutches on a ladder. That dog taught me to make my mind to order my stupid body to go up a ladder. Most tasks are simple when the mind decides that the task is going to be done!

During many of Gen. Patton lectures, he would ask, "Ever watch a cat stretch out after a long snooze? A cat will stretch every muscle as far as every muscle will go. When did you reach as high over your head as you could reach? When did you put your back and head on the floor and stretch your arms and legs as far as you could stretch? Ever try rolling over when your arms and legs are stretched to the limit? Be careful when you do! Could put you in the hospital for a week!"

Gen. Patton's stretching ideas seemed foolish for all of the younger officers. In 1984, over forty-two years after hearing Gen. Patton's advice, I read the advice of Dr. Lawrence C. Lamb in a military journal. Dr. Lamb advised, "If you are going to do heavy labor it is wise to warm up, stretch, work and then stretch again. Everyone needs a daily stretching program that provides a means to stretch most of the major muscle groups in the body!" My mind returned to Gen. Patton and his talking of how cats stretch before starting to move.

Everything Gen. Patton said was geared to combat. I remember one day he shouted to the troops, "Throw away all of your pillows. A pillow takes up too much room in your bedding role. It is worthless! Will not stop a bullet. Keep your head straight so you can get more oxygen into the lungs. Blood will not flow uphill as easily as it will on the level. You elevate your head on a pillow, you are decreasing your brain power. Not enough air can get in your lungs or brain if you use a pillow."

Gen. Patton smiled and the men laughed. His final advice, "If you want to have the brains to think tall, you gotta sleep tall, sit tall and stand tall. To win we got to figure out exactly how we are going to win before we go into combat to kill those bastards!"

During the 1984 Olympic Games in Los Angeles several of the gold medal winners said they won because they "set their minds to win." "Mind-setting" is a new term for the current young generation. Such mind-setting to win is the same as Gen. Patton's principle of making the mind command the body. Gen. Patton gave his mind-setting idea over forty years before the 1984 Olympic Games.

BRAIN POWER COMES FROM THE LUNGS

Gen. Patton did not order any man to stand erect! He explained what happened when the shoulders were kept straight in standing erect.

I remember his lecture on brain power! He said, "In war, as in peace, a man needs all of the brains he can get. Nobody ever had too many brains. Brains come from oxygen. Oxygen comes from the lungs where the air goes when we breathe. This oxygen in the air gets into the blood and travels to the brain. Any fool can double the size of his lungs. Many can more than double their lung power. If you can double your lung power you could be twice as smart and twice as quick. Take ten big deep breaths several times a day. Take in all the air you can get, and then hold that air as long as you can. Air does not cost a cent! It takes brains to think and act quickly to kill the enemy. Try this deep breathing and hold in that air until you pop! This will expand your lungs. Do this deep breathing when you are standing around wondering what to do. No reason for a man to be idle. He can always be doing something such as deep breathing. We are a bunch of lazy breathers. We use our lungs less and less so we increase our dumbness."

"Some of us smoke, like me. I only smoke for promotions and babies. Smoking cuts down on the power of the brain. You can breath deep - every one of you. We want every advantage we can get. We are going to kill the enemy because we will be smarter and quicker on the trigger."

Gen. Patton frequently warned us about smoking too much. I saw him smoke a cigar only one time. He smoked a cigar the day our Intelligence Officer, Col. Pickering, received his star as a General. When Gen.

Patton smoked cigarettes, he held them with two fingers in the style of a college freshman.

Gen. Patton "worked" on those who smoked too much. As usual his advice pertained to combat. I remember him saying, "You never dare strike a match in combat at night. Could reveal our position to the enemy. Many a gun has been fired at a match at night. With powerful field glasses, those matches stand out like search lights. The hot end of a cigarette can cause the loss of several hundred men."

Gen. Patton tried to stop us from smoking, he never issued an order against smoking. If any one of us smoked too much, this officer would feel Gen. Patton's hand on his shoulder, "Sir, you are smoking too much!" Gen. Patton would walk away and never give the officer a chance to reply. The officer had the message.

This lung-oxygen-brain principle was given by Gen. Patton in early 1942. This was at least thirty years before I remember any doctor prescribing oxygen for patients with failing memories. It was at least thirty years before football players used oxygen to give them more power to win.

I have given this deep-breathing principle to luncheon club members. I ask the members of the club to try taking a big deep breath and to hold it until they "pop." After one meeting a doctor suggested that this was dangerous for some people who had never taken a full breath!

When I report this doctor's suggestion to Gen. Patton in heaven or hell, I am sure Gen. Patton will explode, "Deep breathing dangerous? Do the American people use their lungs so little they cannot take a deep breath?"

I try to remember this deep breathing principle

when I get sleepy.   One doctor suggested that deep breathing could add ten years to our lives! I have a friend who is a surgeon.   Every time we meet, he says, "I am taking deep breaths for Gen. Patton."

THERE IS NO POWER IN A
BUSHEL OF BLUBBER

Gen. Patton was not the type of commander who would order men to stand at attention as a type of punishment. When Gen. Patton came into any area soldiers would snap to attention without an order! For all of his lectures and briefing sessions he gave the command, "At Ease!" His instructions on stature were humorous. Although the men laughed, they received the instructions.

He instructed, "Any man who cannot see his shoes without bending halfway to the ground has a real problem! He is spending all of his energy pushing around a bushel of blubber. Every man needs all of the power he can get. Power comes from the engine in the belly. Great piece of machinery that belly. Put in good food and you get good power. If you keep the belly muscles tight you can increase the power of the whole body. I will see that you get the best food I can wrangle out of the Quartermasters. The food you eat turns into power just like putting gasoline in a car. Your belly should be strong and tight enough to take a dozen saber jabs and not stop you from going forward! Do not laugh! You can do it! It has been done! If you can keep going after the enemy has given you several saber jabs, you will scare the hell out of the enemy!"

The men laughed and Gen. Patton continued, "It's no big deal to get more power out of the belly. Just pull it in and hold it for ten seconds. Pull it in ten times every time you think of it. That will give you lots of power. You'll be tuned up like a good engine. A man is a damn fool to die just because he forgot to pull in his bushel of blubber. Every man ought to be able to look down and see his shoes without bending to the ground!

There Is No Power In A
Bushel of Blubber

This principle of strain and pressure was pushed by Gen. Patton before the term, isometrics, became a common word. Everyone laughed at the General, but his words were not wasted. Every man started pulling in his bushel of blubber for the ten seconds. The troops did increase their power! They did stand straight. They laughed at the idea of taking a dozen saber jabs to scare the enemy, but some of them did go ahead after severe injury! The enemy was shocked! So shocked that many thousand of the enemy troops surrendered at the sound of Gen. Patton's tanks.

ASSUMING COMMAND OF I ARMORED CORPS

THE AUTHOR AT ENTRANCE TO HQ I ARMORED CORPS

GEN. PATTON FIRING ON THE PISTOL RANGE

PROFILE TARGETS REPLACED THE CIRCLE TARGETS

THE DAY GEN. PATTON STRAPPED ON THE PISTOLS
JANUARY 15, 1942

GEN. PATTON'S TENT IN THE DESERT

A HEADQUARTERS BUILDING AT DESERT BASE CAMP

INSIDE A BASE CAMP HEADQUARTERS BUILDING

KEEP YOUR FEET CLEAN
AND STUDY THE BIBLE

"It's a hell of a lot more important to keep your feet clean than it is to brush your teeth! You do not walk on your teeth! You use your feet all the time to get at the enemy. Keep your feet clean," Gen. Patton preached.

My feet raised Gen. Patton's anger when I had a severe case of athlete's foot. The California desert sand was always hot, and my feet were so infected that I limped. When Gen. Patton saw me limping and I told him the cause, he exploded, "You are too lazy to bend down and scrub your feet. Bend down there and get all of that crud out from between your toes. Then you will be able to walk." He was right, as usual. Now, every time I take a shower or bath I dig out all of the "crud" as he advised. I have never had a serious foot infection since I followed his advice.

In reading the many books about Gen. Patton, I learned that he continued to push for clean feet during the long drive through Germany in the middle of the cold winter and the Battle of the Bulge. He demanded a new pair of white socks for every soldier every day. He knew the men could not wash and dry their socks in sub-zero weather. The task of getting clean socks to a hundred thousand soldiers would be a task more difficult than my task of getting gas to Gen. Patton's in Carolina in 1941.

This "clean feet" principle does not merit any great amount of attention unless you have sore feet. I associate this principle with the washing of the feet in the Bible although Gen. Patton never mentioned the Bible with his foot-care principle.

He did read the Bible constantly and advised us to do the same. He said so many times, "Read some of the

Bible every day. Study those chapters where it talks about the desert of North Africa. We are going to be fighting in that area. You remember every mountain and water hole mentioned in the Bible. It could save your life! The Bible is accurate. If the Bible tells where there is a source of water, the chances are great a that water hole or spring will still be there."

In the Patton movie a newsman asked Gen. Patton if he read the Bible that was on Gen. Patton's bedside table. The General responded with profanity that he read the Bible every night. In the theater when I saw the movie, the audience laughed at how silly it would be for an army general to read the Bible every night. For Gen. Patton, reading the Bible was not a laughing matter.

Gen. Patton knew the Bible. It is reported that he corrected a high ranking officer of a church on the correct words of a quotation from the Bible which the church officer had used. The church leader reacted to Gen. Patton's correction stating in anger that no man as profane as Gen. Patton should quote any religious verses nor correct a member of the clergy.

Gen. Patton reacted with the same degree of anger, stating that the head of such a great church should not quote false verses from the Bible. Gen. Patton ordered an attendant to get a Bible. Before the attendant could return, Gen. Patton asked the head of the church for the chapter and verse of the quotation the church leader had quoted. The church leader could not give the chapter nor the verse so Gen. Patton walked to the blackboard and wrote the author, chapter and the number of the verse. Turning to the high ranking military officers, Gen. Patton recited the verse. When the attendant brought a Bible into the briefing room, Gen. Patton pointed to the blackboard and ordered the attendant to read the verse from the chapter cited on the blackboard.

As the attendant read from the Bible, it was obvious that Gen. Patton had quoted the verse correctly on every word. The church leader's comment was that he had taken the verse a bit out of context from a more recent translation of the Bible. Gen. Patton smiled and said, "The head of such a great church should never take the Bible out of context!"

This incident has the sound of a legend, but it was reported as a true story in one of Gen. Patton's biographies. I would hesitate to suggest that it might not be true because, as we said so often, the truth about Gen. Patton is usually more amazing than the legends.

I was never able to understand Gen. Patton's unusual memory until I visited with his daughter, Ruth Ellen Patton Totten. She told me that her father had dyslexia. This is the condition in which the eyes and the brain do not work together. Mrs. Totten said, "My father memorized everything because he had problems with reading."

This explained many things for me. Since he had trouble reading the Bible, he memorized the verses so that he would not need to read them again. It also explained why he never used lecture notes when he spoke to the troops and staff. His eyes worked with his brain so improperly that his reading would be too slow to convey the message.

Gen. Patton had a great "RAM," a modern computer term for random access memory. Any weakness of his eyes was offset by his great memory which he could "access" with the speed of a computer.

Gen. Patton thought of the Bible as the best source

of history for the first centuries of our being on earth. A Jewish Rabbi agreed saying, "The Bible was the media of the early centuries. That's the reason for all of the begats and begots. There were people tracing their family trees just as we are doing today."

KEEP MOVING AND PAIN
WILL NEVER HIT YOU

It might be difficult to understand how taking a cold shower could be used to help men go into combat, but Gen. Patton did it. I remember his saying, "Taking a cold shower is just like going into combat. It is only the first second that is hard to take! With a cold shower, if you keep moving around, the pain will not hit you in any one spot. When you go into combat, it is the same way. You keep moving and the enemy cannot hit you. When you dig a foxhole, you dig your grave. In a cold shower, keep jumping around so the little bullets of cold water will spread the pain all over. Hiding in the corner of the shower is the same as hiding in a foxhole. You keep moving and jumping and the pain will be so scattered you won't have it! Same way with the enemy bullets. Keep moving forward and you can find where the bullets are coming from. Then you can kill the bastards. They will be so scared when they see you keep on coming, they will surrender before you get there. It is scary when you know someone is coming to kill you no matter what. And that is exactly what we are going to do! We are going to kill the enemy! No matter what!"

These words lose some of their power without profanity, but the instructions were taken seriously by the troops. We did take cold showers. We did not have a choice! When we moved into the desert in March of 1942 we used the Colorado river water from the Los Angeles aqueduct. The water was ice cold!

The best way to take a cold shower, as Gen. Patton explained, "Is go full-cold at once! Never inch into a cold shower anymore than you would inch up toward the enemy. Dash into the cold shower. Tear into the enemy so fast the bastards will run for their lives!"

Before having any showers in the desert, we had a bucket shower; a bucket with holes in the bottom held up by three poles. It was tricky to warm the water with the sun, cool it with the right amount of cold, throw it into the "holy" bucket, and dash under to get showered before the bucket was empty. As I recall, the engineers built our shower building with five shower heads. When I am asked about well I knew Gen. Patton and how often I saw him, I think of our cold showers and five-hole open pit toilet. We often met in the showers and in the latrine!

Gen. Patton advised taking hot showers for "taking the junk out of the holes in the skin but always finish with cold to close the holes against germs and bugs." Some doctors advise this hot and cold treatment for muscle pain. I still take a cold shower, and it does scatter the pain. I presume the medical principle is the same as putting ice on pain.

Gen. Patton had unusual ideas about body pain. His statements were humorous: "There is nothing new about pain. If you let a little ache or pain drive you to the hospital, you will spend all of your time in bed. More people die in bed than any place! A lot of pains are from sitting in one place too long. Pain has to be shook lose! The body is a machine. Let it set too long and mechanical joints get frozen in position. The way to break out of the pain is to get up and go. Remember in the Bible about the sick man who was told by Jesus to pick up his bed and walk? That sick man did get up and walk away! Pain is just like any enemy. You keep moving around and the enemy cannot hit you. Same way with pain. The quicker you break away from the pain, the quicker you will drive the pain out of your system. You sit too long and you will not be able to move."

When the troops laughed, Gen. Patton would smile and finish by saying, "I am damn sure you will move in a cold shower. Keep moving the same way when the enemy starts shooting."

TO GAIN STRENGTH ALWAYS GO
BEYOND EXHAUSTION

Gen. Patton advocated exercise before the medical profession started prescribing physical activity rather than bed rest for many types of medical problems including surgery. He pushed for vigorous exercise in 1942 long before the surgeons started getting the patients up the day after surgery.

He was preaching exercise before the doctors decided that total bed rest could be final rest in some types of heart cases.

Gen. Patton would advise, "You got to drive the body to the last inch of energy and then go on! You gain nothing by just going up to where your body says you are tired and exhausted. The body will build and grow only to fit the demands which the mind makes upon the lazy body. If all you do is exercise until the body is tired, the body will get lazy and stop a bit shorter every time. You have to go to the point of exhaustion and go on. That way the body will figure, 'We got to build up more body strength if that crazy mind is going to drive this hard.' If you always quit when you are merely tired, you will never gain. Once you let the body tell the mind when to quit, you are whipped for sure. You cannot gain by listening to the body. We can become much stronger if we drive the body."

I remembered Gen. Patton's advice in 1968 when I was on the staff of the Douglas Space Center. One of the doctors in the space program talked of the problems of exercise for astronauts. This doctor stated that research had indicated that muscles will not gain strength by doing something which can be done easily. "To gain strength," the doctor reported, "the body must be exerted to the point of exhaustion and go on." I stopped listening to the space doctor because my mind was returning to the tall figure of Gen. Patton giving the same advice over twenty-five years earlier.

"Every muscle which is not used will start to decline in strength within a few hours after use," the space doctor added. Gen. Patton would have endorsed this idea. I remember his saying so many times, "We can always take one more step! When we are on the attack we can always go one more mile."

Gen. Patton made these statements in 1942. In the 1978 Yearbook of the Illustrated World Encyclopedia, Laurence Cherry stated, "Doctors often unwittingly play the pain game when they admonish the patient to 'take it easy.' And so instead of pushing the body a little more each day, the patient exerts his body as little as possible, getting stiffer and his pain becomes more painful." This article was about pain! Gen. Patton talked of "shaking loose from pain" in 1942. The medical profession started making the same statements over thirty-five years later!

For Gen. Patton it was impossible to go too far. He would say, "We lazy humans only use about a tenth of our total body strength; less than that for our brains. We rust out because we are too lazy to get up a good sweat!"

For those doctors who advise, "Do not overdo," Gen. Patton would protest, "We damn well better over do or we will not do at all!" There is truth in both the doctors' and in Gen. Patton's advice.

Many years later I survived a major heart attack. Gen. Patton's advice was repeated to me by a heart specialist who advised me on how to recover from the heart problem. This advice was completely different from the advice that a doctor had given my father thirty years earlier. My father's doctor had advised, "Take it easy now! Try not to overdo. Get lots of rest!"

My doctor advised, "Getting your pulse rate up to a high of one hundred and fifty is not as important as getting your pulse to a hundred and holding at a hundred for as long as you can. Always try to go a bit further every day to strengthen the muscle of your heart!"

This was the same advice Gen. Patton gave us in his briefing sessions in the Desert Training Center forty years earlier!

Gen. Patton was always driving himself. Every morning in the desert as I pulled myself out of my bedding roll, I could look under the tent flap and hear and see him huffing and puffing as he ran his morning mile. I was twenty-six. Gen. Patton was fifty-seven!

Long after the war I learned that Gen. Patton had competed in the Olympics in 1912. He drove himself to win fifth in the pentathlon. He represented the United States Army and paid all of his expenses to compete. He would have won a medal, but the judges ruled that it was impossible to put two bullets through the same hole in the center ring of the pistol target! The games in 1912 were held in Sweden. Many years later the Swedish government corrected the mistake of the judges and gave Gen. Patton the award that he should have won.

PRIDE IN SELF STARTS WITH
PRIDE IN APPEARANCE

According to Gen. Patton, to be a soldier was the highest goal any man could achieve in life. No man could walk with as much pride as a soldier willing to give his life for his country. Soldiers used the hand salute! Civilians only waved to each other.

In World War I, Gen. Patton, then a Major, demanded a sharp hand salute. This salute was so quick and sharp it became known as the "Patton Salute." In took only one of Gen. Patton's lectures to cause all of the troops to start saluting as soldiers rather than wave a hand to a friend. Soldiers did not "wave!"

I can recall the words of the lecture. Gen. Patton explained - always standing alone with a microphone without a lectern - "We are soldiers! Soldiers do many things immediately and by habit. The most important is the hand salute. Army Regulations say that enlisted men must salute their officers and officers must return this salute. This is a pile of nonsense (not his exact words). Officers can salute enlisted men! The highest profession in the world is that of a soldier who is willing to give his life that others can have better lives. That's the same thing Christ did! Think about that!"

Gen. Patton paused with no change in expression. "Christ had twelve Disciples. Not a damn one of them was a soldier! They all deserted! All twelve of them should have been shot! Every damn one of them! We shoot deserters in this army. We are soldiers. Never forget that you are a soldier. Soldiers salute soldiers. Every American soldier is an army! An army is commanded by a four-star general. Every American soldier is a four-star army because soldiers win wars! Generals cannot win

Pride In Self Starts With
Pride in Appearance

wars. We salute each other because we are all four-star soldiers!"

At the time Gen. Patton was a Major General, the two-star rank. Gen. Patton finished this lecture, as he did with all lectures, by giving the troops a "Patton" salute which he held until the troops returned the salute.

There was no joking with the troops about being soldiers and the salute. The news media joked about the soldiers' saluting. Soldiers saluted! They were four-star soldiers! Gen. Patton said so! They had a war to win, and Gen. Patton said they would win!

Gen. Patton had a clear understanding of fear, faith, and pride. He was constantly striving to kill the fears of every one of his soldiers. Faith and confidence builds pride, and pride destroys fear. No one could build pride in soldiers as quickly as Gen. Patton. The highest tribute any Patton soldier could receive was to be called, "A damn good soldier!" Any man receiving this tribute would swell with pride.

I remember how Gen. Patton instilled pride in every soldier in the Desert Training Center and the I Armored Corps. He did it with his famous necktie order. The Patton critics who made fun of this order in their news stories never understood the full impact of the neck tie. I must admit that when I saw the order I was certain that we were in for trouble.

Before relating the story about the necktie order, a few facts should be stated. I Armored Corps arrived in the California desert without proper uniforms, equipment, tools, or supplies. We arrived with almost nothing for use in the desert. Washing our hands, shaving, washing our feet, and bathing was done in our World War I type metal helmets. This helmet would hold less than a quart of water.

To know the stature of Gen. Patton's reputation, I relate the story of his sending me to a store in San Bernardino, California. My orders were to purchase all of the wash basins which I could find. I remember the shock of the Sears store manager when I answered his question of how many wash basins I wanted to purchase.

I answered, "We would like to purchase a hundred thousand wash basins."

The manager exclaimed, "There can't be that many in the whole United States. People do not use wash basins anymore!"

"We'll buy all that you can locate," I said.

"Who is going to pay for all of these basins?" the manager asked.

"I have authorization from the United States Army and from Gen. Patton on his personal authorization."

"Are you telling me Gen. Patton will pay for a hundred thousand personally?"

"Yes, you can be paid either by Gen. Patton out of his personal account or the United States Army. You can take your choice."

"I'll take Gen. Patton's check! I'll get my money faster. You know he was born near here. There is a town up the road named, Patton."

For the next half hour I listened to legends about Gen. Patton.

With the delivery of wash basins (only a few hundred) to the desert, and with the Army engineers getting water piped to every camp, we could "kick" our helmet bathing. We had showers and toilets at our base camp! No more open pits! We had everything to keep clean and to keep our uniforms neat. We were wearing the summer

101

Pride In Self Starts With
Pride in Appearance

light weight tan uniforms which were not cool but much cooler than the winter uniforms some of us had to wear when we arrived.

I remember the staff meeting which was held a week before the necktie order was issued. Gen. Patton outlined what he desired, "We have reached the stage in our desert training where there is no excuse for any soldier not to be clean and in proper uniform. All of you old officers that have the faded creamy dress uniforms, send those uniforms home and get new whites. If you cannot afford new whites, stay away from our dress functions. I want all of my staff to be in the same color of white! We will not mix our summer tans and dress whites at any function. We are going to have a lot of brass coming out here from Washington to see what we are doing. When we meet with them or with any public organization, we are going to be dressed better than they are. When people come out here at any hour of the day, we will be in the summer tans. Wear only the shirt during the day but put on the blouse in the evening. Army regulations will be enforced. No man, officer or enlisted man, leaves this post without being in proper uniform. And, that uniform better be clean! He must be wearing the insignia of the I Armored Corps on his arm below his left shoulder. Any man out of uniform or with long hair and dirt stays on the post. No man can have any pride if he looks as if he has to go to the bathroom or has just been there!"

Gen. Patton did not say one word about neckties! The necktie was a part of the uniform. There was some complaining from the troops who were turned back at the gate because of dirty shoes, improper uniform, or no insignia of the I Armored Corps.

For soldiers this meant the loss of their three day

pass. The Military Police at the gate did not take any excuses because every man had over thirty days to get his uniform in proper condition.

Gen. Patton knew, as we all did, that a soldier could be in proper uniform when he passed the guards at our main gate and sixty seconds later he could have his tie and shirt off. I must admit I have seen soldiers carrying their shirts and ties as if they were going to the bathroom for a shower.

Gen. Patton's attack on this problem was the necktie order. When I saw the order I was sure we were in for a revolution from the troops. I could see hundreds of men being court-martialed for failure to wear the uniform complete with necktie.

When the order was issued I was the General's Judge Advocate or attorney for the command. I could see the need for a dozen clerk-typists to type all of the charge sheets against the soldiers.

The order was simple. It stated that every man leaving the Desert Training Center would be in proper uniform. There was no mention of having the necktie tied and tucked under the shirt between the second and third buttons of the shirt. The order stated that any officer or non-commissioned officer seeing any soldier out of uniform was ordered to stop the soldier, get his name, and his organization.

This order was for soldiers in downtown Los Angeles, Palm Springs, or any city! If any company commander should have two of his men stopped for being out of uniform off the post in Los Angeles, Palm Springs, or any city, the company commander would be notified and ordered to write a detailed letter explaining why two of the commander's men were out of uniform. This meant that

Pride In Self Starts With
Pride in Appearance

every company commander had to have total "remote" control over his men! Los Angeles was over a hundred miles from our camp.

The necktie order had a third paragraph. If three soldiers from the same company were discovered out of uniform, the company commander would be ordered to submit his letter of resignation from the United States Army or be court-martialed for failure to perform his duties as a commander.

I was correct about one thing. The troops did revolt over the order, but it was not a revolution against Gen. Patton as I suspected. It was a revolution to be neat, clean, and as spit-and-polished as Gen. Patton. Immediately every soldier was wearing the insignia of the I Armored Corps and had the appearance of being ready for a dress parade. Every soldier was walking ten feet tall with the pride of belonging to Gen. Patton!

I talked with many of the company commanders to learn how they had been able to control the soldiers of their command. I learned that the commanders called all of his officers together and declared that before he would submit a letter of resignation, every man in the outfit would be "busted" to a buck private. One commander told me, "I just had a company meeting and said that any man caught out of uniform would be restricted to this desert for the duration of the war!"

I am sure there was grumbling among the men, but the grumbling was slight. When a soldier walked a block in Los Angeles, Palm Springs, or any city, he could see that his dress was so superior to the average soldier that no man in I Armored Corps would ever think of being anything other than "one of Patton's best." There was a revolution in pride. Pride in appearance was the key that

Pride In Self Starts With
Pride in Appearance

Gen. Patton used to build pride in the hearts and souls of the men.

After the necktie order was issued Gen. Patton added a few remarks which I remember. He repeated his "soldier looking like he was coming from the bath room or on his way to the bedroom." He added with his boyish smile, "A good soldier will wait to undress until he gets to the bedroom. He can discipline himself to wait that long! The idea of a soldier looking half-dressed brings disrespect upon the entire United States Army. I do not want any man from our command looking like any other soldier. I want every man to look like he belongs to our I Armored Corps."

In enforcing this order, Gen. Patton did what he always instructed us to do. He enforced the existing regulations and did not enact any new rules. So often some new colonel would insist on writing a new regulation for the troops. After a limited discussion, Gen. Patton would ask, "Colonel, before we do anything let's see exactly what Army Regulations have to say. It seems to me there is a regulation on that. We do not want to confuse the troops with two regulations on the same subject." In nearly every case, Gen. Patton's memory was correct.

Gen. Patton's critics said that the necktie was demanded when on duty under a truck or tank in the field. This was not true. On duty any soldier could wear almost anything which would help him with his work - with one exception - he had to wear the helmet.

Gen. Patton always went into a rage about wearing the helmet. He would shout, "I will shoot any man whether he is dead or not if he does not wear his helmet! That helmet can turn away a lot of junk the enemy might send at us. Wear the helmet at all times. We need every man. We cannot lose any man because he is too dumb to wear his helmet. Learn to work in your helmet! It will save your life."

I remember another lecture that Gen. Patton gave the troops about wearing the insignia on the uniform. We called this lecture, "Let'em know we're comin'!" Gen. Patton always started this briefing with a soft voice with several long periods of silence. He would start by saying, "Before long we will be going into combat. We can hope we will be that lucky! The country needs us to kill those bastards. Combat will be far less exciting than our training here in the desert."

There was laughter. Gen. Patton waited with his boyish grin before saying, "When we go into combat, I will shoot any man that removes the insignia of our organization or the insignia of his rank. I know some generals demand that every man remove all insignia so if captured, the enemy cannot tell what organization they were fighting. I want the enemy to know they are facing the toughest fighting men in the world!"

There was some chuckling, and Gen. Patton would put on his war face and order, "We are the best and don't ever forget it! "Don't let anybody forget that we are the best!"

Everyone was silent as Gen. Patton continued, "I want the rank showing on the helmet on every officer of every rank, officer or non-commissioned officer. Let that rank be seen. Polish that rank on your helmet so it will reflect the light. None of this non-reflective no-polish stuff. When officers are leading the men, the enemy knows they are facing a fighting organization and not a group of men being pushed from behind. Any army with the officers in the rear has all of the fighting strength of a bushel of spaghetti. Enemy troops will surrender when they see our officers are up front!" There was some laughter. "Another thing! Do not worry about being captured. You can be sure you will be treated kindly when you are wearing the insignia of our organization. If you should be captured, tell those bastards that if they know what is good for them, they will surrender because I will never be far away from you."

There was laughter, but Gen. Patton had made his point. There were thousands of Germans who did surrender when they knew they were facing Patton's Third Army. To surrender to Gen. Patton was not as great a dishonor as to surrender to any other organization. Many organizations, according to history, would drive into the area of the Third Army so they could surrender with honor!

One German general, commanding a corps, sent word through the line that he was ready to surrender. To surrender over 20,000 prisoners was not a simple task. Arrangements were made for the surrender terms. On the day and hour assigned the German general made a short speech. The American soldiers who understood German laughed as the other soldiers were silent. The German general had stated that he was surrendering only because he could surrender to Gen. Patton's Third Army! The laughter was caused by the fact that the German general had made his speech in front of troops from the United States Ninth Army!

Gen. Patton's demand for the perfect uniform placed all of us on the staff in unusual situations. For a reception for Gen. Marshall on his visit to the desert, Gen. Patton wanted all of us to wear white gloves. Our staff had increased to over fifty, but only two officers had a pair of white gloves. Gen. Patton contributed two more pair!

In such a reception the officers line up with the highest rank being the first to meet Gen. Marshall. Our reception line went off in perfect style with every officer wearing white gloves! The first colonel to meet Gen. Marshall quickly returned to our line and gave his gloves to one of us who slipped into the "loaned" gloves.

Gen. Patton told us his friend, George Marshall, had complimented him saying, "You always have the most loyal and friendly staff. It is seldom you see staff members greeting each other with so much hand shaking!" We were a "friendly" group of men, but the hand shaking was to exchange the white gloves!

Habits are not easily broken. It has been over thirty years since I tucked the end of the necktie between the second and third buttons of my shirt - to comply with the necktie order. Today, I discover quite often that I have left the second button of my shirt unbuttoned. When I follow this habit, I remember the necktie order and think of Gen. Patton as I fasten the second button.

I live in the southwestern part of the United States where casual dress is common because of the heat. I never wear a shirt without a tie without thinking of Gen. Patton. I puzzle over whether this casual dress causes the lack of pride in self, in family, in schools, churches, and Country. I admit that in the heat of the summer I wear a shirt outside of my slacks. When I do I remember Gen. Patton's remark, "Dressed with your shirt out makes you look like you have just been to the bathroom or have to go!"

A few years ago it was necessary for one of our prisons in a city in Arizona to build a tent outside the jail to house the prisoners. The prisoners shouted, "cruel and inhuman treatment!" The local "no-discipline" society agreed that no prisoner should be confined to live in a tent in the desert.

In the Desert Training Center we lived in tents! Fans and air conditioning had to be installed for the criminals in the tent jail. When discipline fails, pride in self is destroyed. When society does not discipline criminals, criminals punish (discipline) society. When society treats criminals better than they do the soldiers who protect society, pride in self and pride in society is lost.

NEVER FEAR FAILURE

"I've been shot at all of my life. Only once did the enemy ever hit me with a bullet. Of course, I have had a lot of splatter stuff. No matter what you do, people will be shooting at you. Even your friends will shoot at you! It is true you have to protect yourself from your friends more than you do from your enemies! The more you do, the more your friends and your enemies will say you have not done. That's a law of life. If you are afraid of being shot at, you are whipped before you start," Gen. Patton gave this advice to old and new staff members.

I remember Gen. Patton saying, "Men can be divided into two types; command and staff. We always need staff officers, and some men will always be staff types. Some men can never be trained to be commanders."

He lectured on, "We need good commanders. A man is either a commander or he is not. A commander has to lead men into battle. In the history of the world we have had few commanders. It takes the right mixture of common horse sense and stupidity to make a good commander. Smart men know that any battle plan can fail. If I had good sense, for example, I would not be in the Army! But damn it, we've got a war to win. If we do not kill the enemy, they will kill us. War is that simple. It takes a lot of courage to lead men into battles where many of your friends will be killed. A commander does not dare have any fear. If a commander shows any fear, the men will see it. The men will be scared. When there is fear of failure, there will be failure."

It would be many years before I would grasp the full meaning of Gen. Patton's words. I could not believe that some men refuse to make decisions. These are the staff types. These types can never command. Some men do not want the command role where all of the blame will fall upon them for all failures. An example is Bing Crosby who stated on national television that he never wanted a lead role in any movie. He said, "I just want to sing. If the movie flops, I would not suffer too great a loss since I was only the singer."

Our society in 1940 did not want commanders. We wanted followers. We had the gifted child programs. We had the "honors" programs for the children who get high grades from their teachers - with the children graded on their smiles if not with their brains. We taught our children that it was terrible not to have high grades in school. Colleges will not take students unless they have high grades! Our children were smarter than their teachers and the colleges! The children learned that high grades could be secured by merely repeating the words of their teachers. The children took the courses in which they could get high grades without work. Forget the discipline of study to get knowledge; go for the high grades without any work. After a generation we had children who could get high grades but could not face the battles of life - the fear of failure and the troubles of life.

Discipline was so unknown in many schools that some students were "gifted" out of high school - even college - without the ability to read! It reminded me of the briefing sessions when Gen. Patton would discipline a no-discipline officer from Washington. "A dead man does not have any ego," Gen. Patton said so often. High school students dare not be told they did not have enough knowledge to read; would ruin the child's ego to fail to promote him. "Gift" him into the next grade - so he can play football on the team! What is the result? The graduates do not have enough "ego" to read - nor to face life.

Never Fear Failure

I remember a young man who was a "gifted" child in grade school. In high school this young man discovered girls, and the high school teachers discovered that his "gifts" were not in knowledge of his school subjects. His first high school grades were average. His parents could not tolerate having an "average" child! The young man was placed in a private school where he could be protected from failing into average! This young man has never recovered from being "ungifted." He has never been able to face the task of making decisions in the battles of the business world - and of life.

Good commanders must be so stupid that they will attack in the face of fear. Winston Churchill was a fool to say, "We will fight on the beaches, we will fight in the streets and in our homes . . . and though this nation last a thousand years, this will be our finest hour!" Not nice words, but Churchill spoke the truth that the English people had to face the battle for life. Any good staff man would have collected all of the facts about the strength of England and of Germany and said, "We will seek peace in our time." This is an exact quote from the man who was prime minister of England before Churchill.

Hitler expected England to fold and seek peace without a battle. Hitler failed to properly judge the power of Churchill to encourage the English people to accept "nothing but blood, toil, sweat and tears." No doubt Hitler listened to the young men in the university that "resolved not to give their lives for their Country."

A good commander faces the cold hard truth of failure with every decision. He must make decisions without any fear of failure. Gen. Patton charged, "Any officer who is afraid of failure will never win! Any man who is afraid to die will never really live."

"There is a time to take counsel of fear, and there is a time to forget your fears. It is always important to know exactly what you are doing," Gen. Patton admonished.

"The time to take counsel of your fears is before, you make an important battle decision. That's the time to listen to every fear you can imagine! When you have collected all of the facts and fears, make your decision! After you make a decision forget all of your fears and go full steam ahead."

Gen. Patton paused for several seconds before saying, "In war, every plan you make is going to be a life and death decision. You will live or die by your decision. Since we are not afraid of life or death there is no reason to take counsel of our fears."

He continued, ""The chance of being killed in war is not as great as the chance of being killed on our highways back home. If you want to take counsel of your fears, stop driving a car! It is dangerous to charge at high speed towards another car and miss only by a few feet. We do it every day on our highways and accept the fear of a head-on crash. It is not safe to crawl into bed! More people die in bed than any place!" We laughed.

When there was time, Gen. Patton explained his ideas, saying, "The person who cannot face a fear will always be running away from it. If a person cannot face death he will never be able to face life because every day of life is one day closer to death. If you listen to your fears about death you will destroy every day for living!"

I had an experience which proved the wisdom of Gen. Patton's principle of never listening to your fears. I should relate that my service with Gen. Patton ended in

September of 1942. The Army needed pilots, and I was young enough to qualify for pilot training. I should also say that in 1942 all aircraft pilots were a part of the Army Air Corps. The bombers and the fighter squadrons were using the old organization charts which considered aircraft a tool for the Army. We needed every pilot we could get because of the high death rate in the bombing missions over Europe.

One day Gen. Patton asked me to come to his office after a briefing session. He said, "Williamson, I cannot hold you much longer in the Armored Corps. The pressure is on to release every man your age for pilot training. Frankly, we need pilots over us who know something about tanks. There must be close cooperation between the pilots in the planes and the tank commanders if we are to save lives in combat. The only way I can keep you on my staff is if you cannot pass the physical exam for pilot training."

I answered, "General, I passed the flight physical several months ago. I suppose I could dream up some ache or pain and try to flunk a physical. What would you do if you were my age?"

"I would go for the pilot training. The future is in the air. If I were your age? It is not your age, it is the age of your looks. Although you are an attorney, you look too young to ever have a command in the Armored Corps unless the war would last twenty years. Frankly, if you stay on my staff you will be shifted into doing nothing but legal work. You are too young to sit at a desk to fight a war. If I were you I would get the hell out of here! You are sure to get a command in the Army Air Corps despite how young you look. They have generals in the Air Corps that are so young they look like kids! When you get up there do not forget what our tanks look like on the ground!

Don't drop any of your damn bombs on us when you get up there over our heads!"

Gen. Patton was silent for several seconds before rising and putting his hand on my shoulder, "I have just given you the same advice Gen. Pershing gave me in World War I. I was on his Headquarters Staff. He advised me to transfer to the new tank corps rather than shuffle papers on a staff."

Four young officers were transferred from the I Armored Corps to the Air Corps. Several months later I finished flight training and was assigned as a Squadron Commander of one of the first Night Fighter Squadrons; the squadrons using airborne radar. These planes were given the mission of flying at night and in bad weather. Our primary mission was to protect the ground troops at night from bomber attacks. I am sure I was not assigned to this position because of having training with armored tanks, but I do believe I was selected because of service with Gen. Patton. The task was not easy to get pilots to fly at night and in bad weather. Every decision was a life-or-death decision. If the weather was bad, I would make a short flight to get a good weather check for the other pilots. I followed Gen. Patton's advice, "Never ask a pilot to fly when you would not fly!

For an example of using the "never take counsel of your fears" principle, early one morning I was scheduled to fly a P-70 twin-engine Night Fighter aircraft on a test flight with a rebuilt engine. Within a second after raising the landing gear for takeoff, the rebuilt engine exploded. There was no time to take counsel of any fear. Full time was given to keeping the wings level and flying straight. With one engine out, it was the same as one horse pulling and one horse dragging backwards. I was trying to get the plane above the tops of the Florida pine trees and high enough to parachute out or find a suitable spot to crash. I managed to nurse the plane high enough to make a shallow turn back to our own airport. After the emergency landing on the wrong runway I used the good engine to pull the aircraft off the runway. I called the our control tower, "Can you send a tow truck to pull this plane back to the line? I have had some trouble! My right engine is out. I can get off the runway, but I cannot taxi."

The control tower operator did not need to be told that I was in trouble. Earlier I had called the control tower to ask that the field be cleared for my emergency landing. Also, the control tower operator could see black smoke and flames pouring from the right engine.

Following our usual habit when finishing a flight, I reached for the aircraft log book and started to write up the bad engine when the tower operator called, "Don't worry! If you cannot get out of the plane, the ambulance and fire trucks are on the way. They will help you out!"

I came out of my "never-listen-to-fear" state of mind and looked at the flames nearing the gas tanks. It was then I listened to fear and flipped open the canopy and jumped off the left wing without a ladder.

In times of danger from floods, fires, combat, cancer, and old age, the mind does not gain by taking counsel of fears. We will get older whether we listen to the fears of old age or not. The fear of age can be worse than age. Cancer can cause death from worry as easily as from the disease. Proof of this fact is that many people fear cancer so much that they refuse to have the physical examination which could result in early treatment to destroy the cancer.

Several years later, my military service ended with a telephone call from the flight surgeon who said, "We must amputate your left leg. You have bone cancer."

A few weeks earlier a tumor had been removed from my left knee. Cancer had not been mentioned; however, when the slides and x-rays reached Washington, the report changed to cancer. I had been flying again with a metal brace on my left foot. I had just returned to San Francisco from an inspection trip of our radar training center in Florida. War does not provide time for doctors to use good bedside manners. I asked the flight surgeon, "What if I refuse the amputation?"

He did not waste words, "You have less than two years to live even with the amputation."

Having these facts, there was only one decision. With my fellow officers we made up a slogan to laugh at the fear, "Don't hesitate! Amputate!"

Gen. Patton's principles helped me through the amputation. I kept repeating silently, "Never take counsel of the fear of cancer." Every day of life was another day. Every day of life pushed death back one day. No one knows how many days of life we have remaining. Gen. Patton was right. If we take counsel of our fears, we will never enjoy life.

Ten years later the doctor advised, "You have whipped cancer! Most unusual!" Nine more years and a doctor told me, "Something has to go. You have bone cancer again. We have to take off more of your leg or you will go." The surgeons amputated again and left me with only two inches of left leg. The surgeons are still two inches from where I live! This second amputation was over thirty years ago. Gen. Patton's principles have helped me through fifty years of fear!

There are many examples of the wisdom of refusing to take counsel of fear. An example for me is in walking. With the leg amputations I have been compelled to learn to walk with many different legs. Every fitting of a leg requires learning to walk again. With a new leg there is a time to walk carefully watching the wood foot move forward. I learned that if we constantly look at our shoes as we walk, we are sure to stumble and fall. Whether we walk with artificial legs or our own legs, we dare not look at the ground. It is good advice to walk tall. With a wooden leg if I do not walk "tall," the left foot drags the ground. If I lean over to watch to make sure my left foot is coming forward, I stumble constantly. The person with two good legs who looks at the ground will fall more than the "walking-tall" person.

In talking to a large group of troops Gen. Patton would laugh about combat and the fears of combat. "There is nothing to combat! It is just like the fear of getting married," Gen. Patton lectured. "When you have dated every girl in the neighborhood, you have enough sense to get married or stay single. You have the facts! When you get the best combat training and have the best equipment, you are ready to kill the enemy. You can forget your fears and get the job done. There will be a shot that might fall close now and then, but nothing to worry about. Combat is like a marriage. A stray shot now and then is like a spat with your wife - could make the marriage better. The more combat time we can get, the better we will be. Combat will make all of us better soldiers."

There was laughter, but the men learned to silence their fears. Gen. Patton would conclude, "After you make a decision, do it like hell - and never take counsel of your fears."

Gen. Patton had the ability to get to the bare-boned truth, and he gave this truth to the troops. He was blunt, "War means we must kill or be killed. That's all there is to war. If we are to win, we must kill before the enemy kills us."

After his blunt statements, Gen. Patton paused for the truth to "soak" into the minds of the troops. He continued, "In war it is not murder to kill. The declaration of war makes us heros when we kill. War makes it right for strong nations to take over weak nations. Thus, might makes right. "Peace time" religion gets confused about war despite all of the wars in the Bible. Religion gives us a code of what is right, but religion does not have the power to punish the nations that do not do what is "right."

Religion has been causing wars for centuries by starting fights that the religious leaders do not have the "might" to make right. Gen. Washington was said to be "first in war and first in peace." He said, "The way to peace is to prepare for war!" Religious leaders forget that God never wanted people to be weak. The laws of God and of Mother Nature are the same. The strong destroy the weak! This is true in war, true with Nature with weeds, and true with the trees that blow over in the wind. This is God's truth and a basic law of Nature."

Gen. Patton was always talking about the best way to settle a war. His plan was simple, "Let the leader of one country fight the leader of the other country. Think of all the lives that would be saved if only one man had to die from the fight!"

In the early days of our Country the code of honor was to duel with any person who differed with you. The time, place, and weapons for the duel were all set by the "seconds" who had the task of seeing that the duel followed the code of conduct - for the killing. The winner had the "right" to kill. It was a disgrace not to demand a duel or to refuse to duel. This type of killing was permitted by society's code of conduct. This is a basic law of Nature. The buck deer that does not fight for his herd will lose his honor and his herd. The non-fighting buck deer walks away in disgrace and dishonor. The same rule applies to the man in the early years of our Country. The man who refused to duel had to walk away in disgrace as the buck deer walked away.

We stopped our duels after Aaron Burr shot and killed Alexander Hamilton. At the time of this duel, the code of conduct was changing. It was accepted that it was not dishonorable to fire the dueling weapon into the air and not attempt to kill your enemy. According to some of the historians, Aaron Burr failed to follow the new code that required the duel but not the kill. Aaron Burr shot to kill and had to leave the Country in disgrace. The code of conduct was changed to stop duels completely! It was not safe to duel and not know whether to shoot to kill or to shoot into the air!

When nations go to war they are dueling, but they do not have any seconds with enough might to stop the dueling nations from fighting. Poison gas cannot be used, but it is alleged that some nations are prepared to use poison gas. There is a trend towards a code of conduct for nations that would prohibit the use of any weapon that would destroy too many people with one bomb. The problem is there are no "seconds" around to enforce any rule against the nuclear bombs. Unlike the buck deer who can walk away from a fight, nations cannot walk away from attack despite the number of people who are praying and begging for peace.

When At War We Must Kill People

With Gen. Patton's ability to get the truth to the troops, he secured the trust of every soldier. He spoke truth with a forceful attitude whether it was "nice" truth or bad. His constant command to the staff was "get the truth - get all the facts!" His decisions were based on the best information which we could obtain whether it was favorable to our mission or against the mission.

Gen. Patton said so often, "We do not have many good commanders. Not because they all die in combat but because few men can make a decision which could cause their death."

Gen. Patton explained using the example of a pilot flying a plane, saying, "The life of an aircraft pilot depends on his ability to make quick life and death decisions. At the end of the runway before takeoff, the pilot goes through a check-list to make sure the plane is ready to fly. Any mistake in reviewing this check-list and the penalty can be death. Halfway down the runway the pilot must make a second quick decision; namely, is this plane going fast enough to fly or shall the throttle be cut to stay on the ground. The time to make this decision is less than a hundredth of a second. Beyond the half way point on the runway, the pilot cannot change his decision. In fact, he cannot change his direction of flight in case of engine failure; single engine or twin. He cannot change direction until he has a safe speed and altitude. Any attempt to turn back to the airport will result in a crash. This decision-making process must be made so quickly that some men can never learn to fly. They have too many fears of crashing!"

In the evening conversations in his tent, Gen. Patton said, "In life as with flying a plane, some men are never ready for takeoff. Some men want to stay on the ground. Or, should they get in the air, they want to turn back when there can be no turning back. Some men cannot make the life and death decisions required in flying." Gen. Patton often said, "Our fine American young men find it difficult to make the decision to pull the trigger that will kill another man."

It was easy for Gen. Patton to use flying in his examples because he was a pilot. He had his own plane which he flew in the desert. He continued to use his personal plane until the Army secured a plane and a pilot for his use. Whenever there was a need, Gen. Patton did not hesitate to spend his own money to aid the military effort.

I regret to report that Gen. Patton was not a skilled pilot. His landings were so rough that he almost never carried a passenger in the little two-seater plane. The narrow landing strip ran along the Los Angeles aqueduct. The strip was not level, smooth, nor free from blowing sand. Since our tents were not far from the landing strip, it was not unusual for some officer to shout, "He's comin' in!" We ran away from the landing strip - at least far enough so we could watch the landing.

The reason for Gen. Patton's rough landings could have been his eye problems with dyslexia. His eyes could have caused him to be unable to judge the distance to the ground from the air on landing. About his landing of the plane, Gen. Patton would laugh and say, "I always have trouble landing that damn plane. I usually bounce several times. My landings are poor, but my recoveries are good!"

Ministers and laymen who preach so constantly of peace would not understand Gen. Patton and his comparing flying with facing death. However, after Pearl Harbor, we did not have any preaching about peace. Many "peace" ministers joined the Armed Forces as chaplains. They stopped preaching peace and started singing the song,

"Praise the Lord and pass the ammunition." Many ministers learned how to fire all of our weapons of war. Many of them carried the trusty Army automatic pistol on their belt. I remember one saying, "I pray to God to save me, but I know God would want me to do a bit to save myself from the enemy."

Ministers are human, perhaps more human than the average layman. Ministers and preachers can lose their "cool" for peace and change their preaching in a flash. In 1983 a minister's young daughter was brutally raped. In an instant the minster wanted to kill the rapist and would have stabbed the rapist to death if he had not been stopped by friends. In charging at the rapist, the minster was as profane as Gen. Patton.

There is an amusing side to the threat of the nuclear war and the preaching of the peace by the ministers. One of the clergy proposed that "if nuclear weapons could not be banned totally, then, the nations of the world should agree that the nuclear weapons would be used only on soldiers!" This type of thinking places the blame for wars on the soldiers. This type of thinking would blame firemen for fires and police for causing crimes! In truth these preachers are saying, "I am afraid to die! Let some one else die for me!" This violates the teaching of Jesus, "If you are to save your life you must be willing to lose your life."

No one wants to face the truth that the major cause of war throughout the centuries has been religion. In this generation the wars are caused by the constant fighting of the Jews and the Arabs, the Hindus and the Muslims, the Protestants and the Catholics. As Gen. Patton would chide, "No one can argue with God's truth!"

Gen. Patton had harsh words for the religious leaders who opposed the efforts of the military by preaching, "Thou shall not kill." Gen. Patton called these types, "pulpit killers!"

He commented, "These pulpit killers go around preaching that the Bible says, "That you should not kill." This causes the death of many thousands of good soldiers. Damn little these pulpit killers know about the Bible They know even less about the way God works. They should read all of the Bible, not just the part they like. God has never hesitated to kill when one man or a race of people needed to be punished. God helped David kill Goliath! How about Noah and the Ark? All the people were drowned who were not on the ark. God took the blame for this mass murder. How about the opening up of the Red Sea? One race was destroyed and another saved! Don't preach to me about God not wanting us to kill. War means that we have to kill people. That's all there is to it. That is the only way to win. Wars must be won for God's sake! He has a part in every war. The quicker we kill the enemy, the quicker we can go home and listen to the pulpit killers tell us what we did wrong. If it wasn't for us, those pulpit killers would be shot for standing in their own pulpits. Our task is to kill the enemy before they kill us." Usually Gen. Patton finished one of these sessions with a long pause before concluding, "All of this peace talk is the reason our country never goes to war. With the help of the pulpit killers, we invite the attack of the enemy We have invited all of our wars including our first war. We failed to protect our own property so the British moved soldiers into our homes."

Gen. Patton was not as harsh with conscientious objectors as he was with pulpit killers. He accepted the laws which permitted the conscientious objectors to refuse to carry weapons to kill. He advised, "Not every man can be a soldier. To be a soldier is the highest profession of life; comes the closest to being a life like Christ who gave His life for others as we may give our lives in war. When you get a conscientious objector, get him out of the combat unit as fast as possible. If you don't get him out, he will cause many men to die. We dare not hesitate when it is necessary to kill, or we will be killed. We have to be quick on drawing the trigger. Transfer the conscientious objectors and the gold bricks back into civilian life where they cannot cause others to die." "Gold brick" was the word soldiers used for the man who was always showing up on sick call at the hospital.

Although Gen. Patton was critical of gold bricks and pulpit killers, he did not place all ministers in the pulpit idiot or killer class. He invited ministers from the neighboring cities to visit our camp to share church services with our Army Chaplains.

Many accused Gen. Patton of loving war. In fact, the Patton movie script had him saying, "I love war!" Gen. Patton did not love war, but he was proud that he had the faith to face death so that others might live. Gen. Patton hated war far more than the pulpit killers. Often he quoted the Bible, "We will always have wars and rumors of wars." Gen. Patton hated the military and political leaders who delayed, regrouped, consolidated gains, defended land, dug foxholes, or would do anything that would make the war last longer than necessary. His first thought was always about the soldiers and how to save their lives.

For some men war is a political game. It is necessary to keep military generals and political leaders happy despite the cost in the number of soldiers killed on both sides of the war. A British General, H. Essame, reported, "Four times since the break out at Avranches (invasion of France), Patton and his Army gave

When At War We Must Kill People

Eisenhower opportunities which might well have proved decisive, shortened the war, saved thousands of lives and left the West in a better strategic posture than it would be more than a quarter of a century later!"

It is so easy to think of war as the draft, the training, of building planes, moving men and materials, and even of helping the economy of the country. It is so easy to forget that the primary mission in war is to kill the enemy.

The war with Japan ended immediately after the nuclear bomb was dropped. We can hope that the society of nations will decide that nuclear bombs kill too many people. The result could be international peace!

GRAB'EM BY THE NOSE
AND KICK'EM IN THE PANTS

Gen. Patton's best known principle was "Grab'em by the nose and kick'em in the pants." These words are simple, but few management experts or military commanders understand the importance of this principle.

Gen. Patton's words were blunt when he spoke to the soldiers. "We are in war. Wars are won only by killing people. It is easier to kill people when you can see what you are shooting at. That's for sure! Planes and big guns can drop bombs and shells on the enemy or behind the enemy lines. This does not do much good in killing people. Not many soldiers can be killed by scaring them to death. We got to go up and grab the enemy by the nose. We will go where we can see the enemy. We will let the enemy know we are not afraid. We will let them know we are coming for only one reason; to kill them. When we grab'em by the nose they will shoot at us. That is just fine because from their firing we know where they are. We will move so fast they will not hit us. After we get the attention on their nose, they will keep shooting at where we have been. We will move around behind them with our tanks and capture all of their gas, food, and supplies. We will kill every one that gets in our way."

Gen. Patton would pause before adding, "We'll even capture all of their women!" He spoke the words the solders understood. "We'll always move fast. We'll never dig foxholes to hide in. When you dig a foxhole, you dig your grave! When you are in that foxhole and fire at the enemy, the enemy knows exactly where you are. They will soon get you in their gun sights and you will be dead. You keep movin' and you'll never be in the enemy's gun sight!"

Grab'em By The Nose
and Kick'em In The Pants

Gen. Patton would close with his usual words, "Remember, wars are won by killing people. The more we kill, the quicker we'll get out of this war. Wars are not won by defending land. Let the enemy have any land he wants as long as we can get him into a position where we can kill him."

In World War II many generals attempted to fight the war on the principle of defense. Few generals used the principles of speed and movement. Most of the generals used the principle of position.

Gen. Patton always wanted the best position where he could destroy the enemy; this was usually behind their line of defense. Gen. Patton's principle was that the enemy had to be kept under constant attack. To defend a position would mean the enemy was able to get into an attacking position.

For an example, in Viet Nam we never "grabbed the enemy by the nose." We never knew why we were in Viet Nam. Killing people was not the objective. I remember hearing a service club speaker, a high government official, say that a little bit of war in a distant place was good for the economy of the United States.

Fighting a war to help the economy would cause Gen. Patton to explode, "Who in hell ever heard of fighting a war to help the economy? War is killing people. Trying to say there is such a thing as a little bit of war is like trying to say a woman is a little bit pregnant! Who would have the gall to tell a soldier he was giving his life to help the economy?" There are many practical examples of the need to grab a problem by the nose and kick it in the pants. The discipline of children requires the prompt action of facing the enemy, the child that needs discipline.

Too often the mother will say, "You have disobeyed

again! Wait until your father gets home. He'll give you the punishment you deserve." When the father comes home, he may say, "Let's wait until morning. We might cause our child to lose sleep tonight. Let's wait and see if he does it again."

Too often this delay gives the child the chance to take all of the "attack" positions so that he can demand the surrender of his parents. The child that is grabbed by the nose and spanked in the pants will appreciate that the parents are teaching the child how to make the mind control the body.

When parents fail to discipline children, the children lose respect for authority from any source whether it is home, school, community, or society. These children may refuse to register for the draft and to serve their country. Or, as Gen. Patton said so often, "In the United States, we always invite the enemy to attack by our refusal to face the threats of war."

Those in fear of retirement and death fail to grab the "enemy" (death) by the nose and destroy the fear. Too often retirement hits like a surprise attack from an enemy. Few people grab retirement by the nose. Many of us do not catch the principle that every day of life is one day closer to retirement. Every day of life at any age is one day closer to death. Failure to grab death by the nose can cause us to live our last years in constant fear. When our life expectancy is down to a few years, the enemy (death) may be in total command. When death is "grabbed by the nose," we are not in a "foxhole" of depression over death.

Gen. Patton's simple principle is so easy to state but difficult to live. Many organizations never actually grab the enemy (local problem) by the nose. Many governmental agencies never grab their mission by the nose. Too often their primary mission is to make sure they continue their government program for another year. Keep the problem unsolved! Never grab it by the nose!

I am not sure that Churchill ever caught the importance of speed in winning wars. Churchill's personal physician did not understand the importance of Gen. Patton's principle when he wrote in his book, "Patton was an unusual general; he was not much good at fighting a battle, but he was the best pursuit general of recent years. If Monty (British General Montgomery) had been as good in pursuit as he was in fighting a battle, then he would have been one of the great captains."

Fighting a battle as Churchill and Montgomery wanted to fight was exactly what Gen. Patton wanted to avoid. Gen. Patton would say, "It's a waste of our fine young men to stay in fixed positions and see who can send over the most shells. It costs too many lives to stay in foxholes where the enemy can keep firing until they bracket into a perfect shot. We must keep moving and let the enemy hit where we have been. Let the enemy stay in their fixed positions. We will move fast and destroy the enemy as they prepare to 'do battle' with us. This is the way to win the war. Always keep the enemy 'defending.' Never let the enemy pick the battle site. We will fight where we want to fight and not where the enemy wants to fight. We will always keep the odds of battle on our side."

This principle is discussed in the chapter on the rules for winning. Gen. Patton would never fight the day-in and day-out battle of merely sending shells at the enemy. He did not want to destroy a bridge or road that could be used in pursuit of the enemy. Montgomery, by his own statements, always wanted to regroup, consolidate gains, or wait for reinforcements.

Grab'em By The Nose
and Kick'em In The Pants

So often Gen. Patton would order, "To hell with taking three days to regroup! We will regroup on the run. Let the women and children consolidate our gains. When we get the enemy on the run, we must keep him on the run. We must run faster than he does! We'll not need food when we are winning! We will eat the enemy!" Harsh words but the soldiers caught the principle. The enemy can not kill when the enemy is on the run."

Many military and management leaders fight their battles on the principle of maintaining positions. So many workers in large corporations consider the coffee break as the major mission of the day. So few understand Gen. Patton's principle of how to grab the problem by the nose and work to solve the problem. Few of us grab our problems by the nose and kick the problem in the pants!

MAN IS THE ONLY WAR MACHINE

Gen. Patton constantly stressed that "man is the only war machine." In his lectures and in the staff meetings he said, "All this talk about super weapons and push-button warfare is a pile of junk. Man is the only war machine. Man has to drive the tanks, fly the planes crawl, through the mud, pull the triggers, and push the buttons. We will train to be strong in body and mind. Always remember that man is the only machine that can win the war."

No general I ever knew had such a clear picture of war and the necessity of training for combat. We smiled at Gen. Patton's simple ideas, but the ideas were sound.

"It's nice to have good equipment," he lectured. "A tank is a great weapon for killing infantry troops. So is the machine gun. But man is the key. Remember the French Revolution? The battles of that war were won with brooms, sticks, and stones - by a bunch of angry women. Get a determined bunch of men and women, and they will win the battles no matter what the odds or what kind of equipment they use. We won the Revolutionary War, didn't we? It was against a far superior military force. Remember what they used in the first battle? They cut logs and rolled them down the hill at the enemy. Rolling logs did not kill, but it sure scattered the British troops so they could not fire their muskets."

If some exhausted officer would fall asleep during a long lecture, Gen. Patton would go to the officer. With his hand on his shoulder, Gen. Patton would ask, "How long you been without sleep?

If the officer reported anything less than forty-eight hours, Gen. Patton would go into a rage about staying awake for at least two days when in combat. If the man had not had any sleep for more than two days, Gen. Patton would order him to leave and get to sleep.

"You give me ten good men not afraid to die, and we will destroy an enemy division of ten thousand. That is, if the ten men will stay awake." Gen. Patton smiled.

One of Gen. Patton's greatest talents was the ability to destroy fear in the minds of the soldiers. He eliminated fear in his own mind and gave the same ability to the troops. He considered fear the first enemy that had to be "killed." "Face every fear and every fear will disappear," was a basic principle for him.

One day after one of these lectures, Gen. Patton added, "I should say that our first enemy will always be Congress. Congressmen are always running for reelection. Money for defense comes only after election. We have to live with Congress."

Gen. Patton's most famous anti-fear speech was called, the "blood and guts lecture." Within hours after new troops were under Gen. Patton's command, they would get the blood and guts speech. Usually this speech was given to large groups of at least two hundred men. Gen. Patton would stand on any elevated mound of sand in the desert. He used a floor mike. He stood as straight as the iron pipe holding the microphone. He never touched the iron pipe for support. He did not use any notes nor index cards. He never "read" a prepared text. Staff officers were ordered to attend every lecture so that we could get the reaction of the troops. I regret that I did not tape this lecture. I have not been able to locate a printed text of the speech.

I heard this "sermon" so many times I can report most of his words from memory without missing many words. The profanity I will not attempt.

Gen. Patton would give a loud command, "At

ease!" He would wait for several seconds wearing his most severe war face. When every soldier was completely motionless, He lectured, "Soldiers, do not worry about being scared when we go into combat. Any man who says he is not scared is a damn liar. I know. I've been in combat, and I've been scared. Now, I can tell you when you will stop being scared. When the first shell hits near you, that's when you will stop being scared. You take your hand and wipe your forehead. On your hand you will find the blood and guts of your best friend - you stop being scared. You'll know exactly what to do. You will kill those bastards that killed your best friend - before they kill you. That's war. You either kill or get killed. Never worry about being scared. You will know what to do."

It was a short lecture. Almost too short for the massing of the troops, but the words would stay in the minds of the soldiers. Gen. Patton would march to his command car or jeep and drive away. Other officers would dismiss the troops.

We called this lecture, the "gory" lecture, but the blood and guts frankness gave the troops the true meaning of war. The troops stopped being scared. If Gen. Patton would admit being scared, they could be scared.

The newsmen called Gen. Patton, "Old Blood and Guts" and wrote, "It's the blood of the troops given for Patton's guts." We did call him this at times, but it was for the sermon and not for ordering the troops into foolish battles. On any battle and at any moment, Gen. Patton would appear with the troops in the thick of enemy fire. He faced the same fears the soldiers faced.

In addition to this sermon, Gen. Patton used every trick in the book to build confidence in the troops. The pearl-handled pistols (we always called them pearl) were symbols to destroy fear and build confidence in the minds of the soldiers. I remember the first day he wore the pistols. I had a camera and took his picture. It was a chilly winter day in January, 1942. We had received a few hand guns (45 automatics) and some ammunition so we were on the small arms range at Fort Benning, Georgia. As a junior officer, the only equipment I had was an empty pistol holster and camera. Higher ranking officers had the pistols and fired at the targets before the lieutenants could take practice shots. In January for the target we had the large circle with the center dot. Gen. Patton changed these targets to the shape of a man in the enemy uniform.

When the others were firing I was with Col. Gay who saw Gen. Patton's pistols and asked, "General! Where did you get those fancy pistols?"

Gen. Patton answered, "I shot a Mexican general out of his saddle when I was with Gen. Pershing in Mexico chasing Pancho Villa. Ask me what I'm going to do with these pistols?"

"What **are** you going to do with them?"

"I'm going to shoot that son-of-a-bitch Rommel and throw these pistols in his face!"

This story was told and retold many times. I did not believe the saddle shoot-out story. In fact, I never made any study of Gen. Patton's World War I experience. Several years after World War II, I was introduced to a retired soldier who had been the driver of the automobile from which Gen. Patton fired at the Mexican general. The driver related the story, "We were driving by a deserted ranch house. It was a rough road for our auto. Suddenly, this horse and rider came from behind the house shooting at us. Patton ordered me to stop the car. I put on the brakes but before I could get stopped, Gen., Patton was outside standing on the running board firing across the top of the car. His first shots killed the man who fell off of his horse. We could see he was a general. We strapped him on the front hood of the car as you would a buck deer and drove back to Gen. Pershing's headquarters."

Gen. Patton's pistols created more international confidence than Churchill's two-finger salute with the "V and words 'when you die take one of the enemy with you." Within a few weeks the "V" was changed to victory. People did not want the truth that the price of victory could be at the cost of their own death. Gen. Patton would never let the troops forget that the price of victory in any battle was the killing of the enemy. Every soldier knew the fancy pistols were going to kill Rommel. Later, Gen. Patton said he was going to kill that SOB, Hitler. The soldiers knew Gen. Patton would do it!

Gen. Patton used every method to build confidence in the soldiers to kill. During the day he drove in an open jeep among the troops as he advanced towards the enemy lines. The staff made plans for a small plane to land on a road or in a field near the front. At dusk, Gen. Patton would meet the plane and pilot and return to his headquarters by air so that the troops would never see him retreating. Gen. Patton wanted the soldiers to always see him going to the front lines.

IN THE LONG RUN, IT IS WHAT WE DO NOT
SAY THAT WILL DESTROY US

I doubt that Gen. Patton was the first to state that failure to speak could cause destruction, but he constantly followed this principle. He spoke the truth when the leaders in public life would stay away from truth. He violated all of the rules in current use, such as: "Don't make waves. Do not fight city hall. Keep your mouth shut and you'll stay out of trouble. Never speak if it will create ill will. Right or wrong, stick with the establishment." This type of action was not for Gen. Patton who never hesitated doing everything he could to irritate an enemy, foreign or domestic.

Gen. Patton's attacks upon false idols and ideals caused all of the staff to worry when he spoke in public. He never hesitated to grab a problem by the nose and shake out the truth. I remember his saying, "This war was caused by every last one of us. No one spoke out against Hitler. Everybody wanted peace in their own lifetime. If any leader of any country had opposed Hitler, we would not be fighting this damn war. Only Churchill spoke out against Hitler, but Churchill's election as Prime Minister of England came too late to prevent the war. It is what we did not say that is destroying us now. In trying to buy peace for our lives, we will pay the price of losing thousands of our finest young men."

I remember a colonel who suggested that Gen. Patton tone down his remarks about our war policies. This colonel was trying to be helpful and suggested that there was merit in the old motto, "Speak no evil, see no evil, and hear no evil."

Gen. Patton went into one of his impromptu briefings, "Yes, colonel, but that "no evil" business is for

In The Long Run, It Is What We Do Not
Say That Will Destroy Us

monkeys who hide their eyes, ears and mouth to the truth! God is truth and don't ever forget it! Evil must be attacked whenever it appears. You hear your kind of garbage every day, but let me tell you something. It is foolish to say that you should never get into a professional contest with a skunk. I will tell you that if you do not kill the first skunk that shows up, that skunk will get under the house and you will have to burn the house down to get rid of the skunks." These words are not exactly what Gen. Patton said. He used profanity to give his words more meaning!

There was laughter and when the laughter stopped, Gen. Patton continued, "Look at Pearl Harbor! No one wanted to get into war. We said so! Any fool could see it coming. We invited the attack! We let the skunks get under our front porch, and so we burned at Pearl Harbor!"

Many years later I remembered Gen. Patton's "speaking-out" principle when a service club adopted a four-way test for truth as a way to avoid troubles and keep "peace." This four-way test was as follows: Of the things we think, say or do,

1. Is it the truth?
2. Is it fair to all concerned?
3. Will it build goodwill and better friendships?
4. Will it be beneficial to all concerned?

I know how Gen. Patton would attack such a test. He would explode, "Who in the hell do those people think they are that they can pussy-foot around with truth? God is truth. Never forget it! You take some pussy-footin' test in war and you are dead! What a damn fool Patrick Henry was to say, 'Give me liberty or give me death!' Such a statement makes fools out of every man who signed our Declaration of Independence when they 'pledged their lives, their fortunes and their sacred honor!' We would not have this Country if John Hancock had been a member of that service club. Can you imagine John Hancock saying, 'I am signing my name big enough so the King can see it, but first I want to be sure this Declaration of Independence will build goodwill!' Starting our Revolution did not generate friends nor build goodwill, and it was not beneficial to all concerned!"

"Pussy-foot" was a term Gen. Patton used for delays. I am sure Gen. Patton would continue with humor and not with rage about such a foolish four-way test for truth. He would smile and say, "If Noah had been a member of such a service club, he would have answered God by saying, 'Before I can lay down the first plank for the Ark, I will have to take a four-way test. God, please tell me! Will a flood benefit everybody and make friends?"

All of our training in the military, in our schools and churches is to believe in ideals, to stand for something and to have faith in God. When we do not speak out in support of the Founders of our Country, we destroy our Country!

Should there be any doubt that this four-way truth test is a "silencer" of truth, one of the international presidents of this service club told me, "Yes, that four-way test conflicts with our ideals of service, but I cannot say anything about it. It is too well established in our thinking!"

When we establish false ideas in our clubs and in our minds that degrade our patriotism and religious beliefs, we follow a course of destruction. When we have fears of speaking the truth, we lose faith in our basic beliefs. Neither God nor truth can be pussy-footed away, using Gen. Patton's term.

Current examples of our "destruction" is in our

In The Long Run, It Is What We Do Not
Say That Will Destroy Us

giving the Pledge to the Flag and to the Republic for which it stands and singing the Battle Hymn of the Republic. As we give lip service to our Republic, our political leaders attempt to sell democracy to us and to other countries. It is true that in a democracy the people are all powerful or sovereign; however, this power does not come from the people every hour of the day. The power of the people is to be used only on election days. When this power is used only on election days, we have a Republic. When the people want to "vote" every day on every bill in Congress and on every act of the President, we have a true democracy.

When our society enjoys taking polls on the people on every nit-picking question, it is a democracy. Such a democracy keeps the people happy and keeps re-electing the non-thinking representatives for our government. These types are serving the people and not the Country. It is so easy to see these problems if we can stretch our minds as Gen. Patton did to see several thousand years instead of some personal penny-gain at the end of our noses.

Listen to one of our Army Generals of the early thirties, Gen. C. P. Summerall, "One of the earliest forms of government, and one of the worst forms, was the true democracy, in which every question was submitted to the will of the people. We see outbursts of this even in our own day (1933) in what is known as mob rule. It naturally and inevitably degenerated into demagoguery!" Gen. Summerall held the office of Secretary of War when we had a War Department. We now have a Department of Defense, a term which Gen. Patton would never approve!

If you should think that Gen. Summerall is wrong, listen to the historian, Thucydides, writing about four

In The Long Run, It Is What We Do Not
Say That Will Destroy Us

hundred years before Christ was born, "Democracies always self-destruct because the people will spend into bankruptcy!" As our current Congress debates our deficit, we are about three thousand years out of date. We do not want truth! This power of the people struck me one morning when I was in the Oval Office of our White House with the President and his Executive Aide. I had the evidence to prove an assistant to one of his cabinet members was breaking basic rules of our Constitution. I was pleading with the President to fire the responsible cabinet officer. The President's reply was a shock, "We would not dare touch that question at this time. The news media would kill us." An amazing admission by one who has the might of our Country in his hands!

I should include a remark which the President added; namely, "Never forget that every single citizen in the United States has more power than I have as President."

A truth which we should speak - and keep repeating - is that we elect our representatives to serve our Country; not to go to Washington to get re-elected! Failure to speak such truth has destroyed our credit position with a staggering national debt.

There was a day in our history when President Monroe told the world that we would go to war if any nation made any attempt to move into any country in our part of the world. That day is gone. Today, the best way to get elected to office is to promise "Our soldiers will not fight on foreign soil. We do not want war." Every little kid knows that the best way to get into a fight is to constantly cry, "I am afraid to fight!" Our first President, Gen. Washington cautioned, "The way to have peace is to prepare for war." Gen. Patton would be so proud that

In The Long Run, It Is What We Do Not
Say That Will Destroy Us

Gen. Washington did not say, "Prepare for defense!"

Gen. Patton was considered a rash, outspoken reckless military type who wanted war, but war was what Gen. Patton believed could be prevented by having faith to keep up defenses so that we need not fear attack from any enemy.

I remembered Gen. Patton's principle about the power of silence to destroy when the Watergate explosion hit the newspapers. In addition to all of those who were directly involved and went to jail, how many hundreds had knowledge of the illegal acts and said nothing. How easily Watergate could have been avoided if the skunks had been stopped before they dug under the front porch - of our White House.

This principle is as valid today as it was during Gen. Patton's life. In fact, this principle was quoted almost in the exact text by one or our State Department diplomats during the England-Falkland fighting. This envoy said, "When any relationship turns sour, it's usually because of what was not said, not what was said!"

Argentina assumed that we would do nothing to help England. Argentina assumed that we wanted "peace at any price." In truth, as Gen. Patton said so often, "We invited the war!" We did not actually engage in the Falkland affair, but we gave support in many ways - ways which Argentina did not expect.

As history is being written, Gen. Patton's principles are proving to be correct. Respect for Gen. Patton is growing throughout the world with over twenty-five memorials dedicated to him in Europe. Many of the military and political leaders who opposed Gen. Patton have been forgotten or have lost respect. In 1945 Gen. Patton was relieved of command for being so rash as to

142

In The Long Run, It Is What We Do Not
Say That Will Destroy Us

say, "We must build up Germany as a bulwark against Russia." That rash statement of 1945 is a basic policy of our government today. As usual, Gen. Patton was thirty years ahead of the leaders. The leaders who remain silent when they should speak are soon lost from memory.

President was not silent when Russia needed to be called an "evil empire." Reagon also spoke out in saying, "Take down the Berlin Wall."

The wall came down! Before President Reagon spoke out against Russia, we were in fear of the military might of Russia.

TALK WITH THE TROOPS

The stories are numerous about Gen. Patton talking with the troops. Most of the stories are true; some are legends. The most amazing stories are true! I remember an incident which happened when we moved into the Desert Training Center. Gen. Patton spotted a man working on a telephone pole near our camp. This man was wearing Army tan pants, but his shirt was an off-color tan; plus the man was wearing a large plantation straw hat. Gen. Patton was rough on men being out of proper uniform. We were supposed to wear the fiber liners for the steel helmets! We had not received the new metal helmets. Gen. Patton ordered the man to climb down the pole. The man gave some short greeting and ignored Gen. Patton's order.

Gen. Patton shouted, "Come down from that pole! I am ordering you down from that pole. You are out of uniform!"

"I cannot take time to come down, and I don't know what your problem is but I can't listen to you. I got work to do."

"You come down or I'll shoot you down! You have disobeyed my order. I have the right to shoot you when you disobey an order!"

The man continued to work, answering, "You shoot me down, and you will go to jail for murder. The only man who can order me off this pole is my telephone supervisor. He'll shoot me if I don't get this job done this afternoon."

Gen. Patton smiled, "You with the telephone company?"

"Right! We have some mad general coming in here with a big army. They want hundreds of lines hooked up all at once. I wish you would just go on about your business so I can finish this splice."

Gen. Patton laughed, "Carry on! I thought you were a soldier under my command. Those tan pants fooled me. Get your work done. We need telephones. I'm the mad general your boss wants to avoid!"

The man looked down and mumbled, "For Christ's sake!"

Gen. Patton answered, "No! It is not for Christ. It is for me and our soldiers that we need telephone lines."

One morning I was riding with Gen. Patton in the desert. We were about thirty miles from base camp. Gen. Patton was surveying the desert with his field glasses watching the movement of the tanks and supporting equipment. He spotted a truck on the paved highway several miles away. During the desert maneuvers no army vehicle was permitted on the highway. Every vehicle had to move on the desert sand. It was over ten miles to the highway, but Gen. Patton ordered the driver to chase the slow moving truck going back to base camp on the highway. When we caught the truck, Gen. Patton waved the driver to the side of the highway.

"What's the problem, soldier? Can't you take the desert? You know the orders! No vehicle is permitted on the highway during maneuvers," Gen. Patton was wearing his war face.

"General, I can take the desert, but this truck cannot. I am trying to save the transmission by limping back to base. You want to know the problem? I'll tell you. You keep asking for more men and equipment to get into the desert. My commanding officer keeps trying to keep you happy by sending out all the equipment that'll run. Well, if we lose many more trucks we will not have enough equipment to haul our rations back from Indio. I don't look forward to walking to Indio and bringing rations back in a hand basket!" The soldier was as disgusted as Gen. Patton was angry.

"You still having problems getting parts?" Gen. Patton asked.

"No change. We cannot make repairs without repair parts!"

"What's the problem with your transmission?" Gen. Patton was relaxed.

"General, they don't make a transmission for this desert heat. Somehow we got to get a cooler in front of the oil pan or the transmission will always burn out!"

Before we drove away, Gen. Patton gave the soldier a drink from his canteen and congratulated the soldier for caring more for his truck than he did for obeying orders of superiors. To be offered a drink from Gen. Patton's canteen was an award equal to the Distinguished Service Cross! We discussed the cooling problem, and I was ordered to get all the facts and write a report for Washington. While were still in voice range, Gen. Patton said, "That man is one damn good soldier." The soldier beamed with pride.

Women were not spared from Gen. Patton's wrath although they were not in the Army. Gen. Patton saw a car on the main highway with a flat tire as we were returning to our base camp after a maneuver. The car had a Georgia license plate. Georgia was our "home" when we were stationed at Fort Benning. A soldier in uniform was helping the woman change the tire. The woman was in extremely short shorts, and women did not wear such shorts in 1942. Gen. Patton assumed that the woman was what he called, "a camp follower." Gen. Patton ordered his driver to stop.

Gen. Patton started, "Soldier, why are you leaving

your duty assignment to help this camp follower who belongs back in Georgia?"

"I don't have to report in for duty assignment for three more days. And this woman is not a camp follower. She is my wife."

Gen. Patton apologized, and offered to help with changing the tire. We stayed with the couple until they could drive away.

Gen. Patton would not tolerate any abuse of his men. In the first weeks of our being in the desert we were visited by many from Los Angeles and Hollywood. It was good publicity for movie stars to have their pictures taken with soldiers and tanks. Every one wanted to get into the war! We had some beautiful young starlets visit our camp with their agents and photographers. These young girls excited the troops! Several of the young starlets gave their telephone numbers to some of the men.

I learned several weeks later how much "service" the young girls gave. One of the young officers on our staff confided that he had to get five hundred dollars to one of the girls for an abortion. As the Judge Advocate for the staff, I advised that he should offer to marry the girl. She refused stating that marriage would "compromise" her career. I advised that he should be the dutiful lover and go with her for the abortion and give the money directly to the doctor. This was not acceptable to the girl. As I was attempting to help this man, two others came in with the same problem. On questioning I discovered that the same girl was asking for "fatherly" help from all three of the men for the same abortion!

Since this was a problem which could exist without Gen. Patton's knowledge, it was decided to bring the problem before the full staff. Gen. Patton solved the problem in a few minutes. Gen. Patton ordered that no man could get married without talking to a chaplain. All of our chaplains were alerted to the extortion schemes. In addition, Gen. Patton ordered that no more women of any type would be permitted in camp. This included wives, girl friends, mothers, and relatives. In truth, the desert was not a decent place to visit with any one. If a family member or relative wanted to visit a soldier, the soldier was given a three day pass to enjoy the visit away from the desert.

One exception was made to this order. Gen. and Mrs. Marshall came to visit one of our maneuvers. Since Gen. Marshall was the Chief of Staff for the President of the United States, an exception was made by Gen. Patton! Mrs. Marshall and Mrs. Patton were good friends; hence, both wives came to the reviewing tent. This is the only time I ever saw Mrs. Patton in the desert. I saw Gen. Patton every day. I have read reports that Mrs. Patton was always visiting our desert camp carrying a white umbrella. The day she was with Mrs. Marshall, neither wife was carrying an umbrella as the photo in this book will indicate. Gen. Marshall, Mrs. Marshall, and Mrs. Patton came in a four-door sedan. Their car was driven within ten feet of the reviewing stand. An umbrella would not have any value in giving protection from the heat. The desert sun and heat was such that any frail umbrella would give almost no protection from the sun. A tent was constructed to protect Mrs. Marshall, Gen. Marshal, and his Washington staff. Gen. Patton always stood outside of the cover of the tent! Gen. Patton would never stand in the shade when his men were out in the blazing sun.

One time I was asked if we used big fans to keep cool when the temperature went so far over a hundred degrees. I gave a truthful answer despite how foolish it sounded. I answered, "No, we do not have any fans. We roll up the sides of our tents!" That was all we could do to keep cooler.

I did not hear a single complaint over Gen. Patton's order keeping women out of the desert. Many were grateful to have three days rather than a few hours with their family. This order keeping women out of the camp was not as harsh as it might seem. There is nothing comfortable about "visiting" with any friend in the shade of a tent when the temperature was often above one hundred and twenty degrees.

In staff meetings, Gen. Patton instructed, "Take time to talk with the troops. They know more about the war than anybody. Far more than we do! Make them tell you all of their gripes. Let them know we are doing everything we can to help them. Let the soldiers know they have to win the war. Tell them the truth that they are the most important part of the Army. They will not trust you if you do not trust them."

Gen. Patton walked back and forth in silence. He knew his little silent walks in front of the staff had great impact. He finished saying, "Always remember in talking with the troops the most important thing to do is to listen!"

Gen. Patton was concerned about every man of every rank. He was always talking with the soldiers. He touched soldiers with a hand shake or a slap on the back. No man was so dirty or greasy that Gen. Patton would decline to shake his hand. The orders were that all officers were saluted with the hand salute by every soldier. The soldier saluted first and held the salute until the officer returned the salute. Gen. Patton did not hesitate to salute the soldiers before they saluted him. If a man deserved a compliment, Gen. Patton would snap to attention and salute the man for his work. When we were in the desert with all of the dust and dirt, I have seen soldiers try to stand in a straight-line formation and salute Gen. Patton when he drove past their area. For Gen. Patton the salute was something which only soldiers exchanged. Gen. Patton wanted every soldier to salute with pride!

Gen. Patton did not require the troops to do anything which was not essential. We did not hold any parades to march past a reviewing stand. Such parades did not have any value in tank wars. Every meeting of a large number of soldiers would be with Gen. Patton on parade. He would stand in front of the soldiers and talk to them about the objectives of a battle plan and how to stay alive.

I remember a colonel who wanted to start rifle drill teams with competition among all of the military organizations for the best drill team. Gen. Patton denied the request, saying, "Rifle drill teams are for peace-time armies when the troops have little to do. We have a war to win. I do not want any man using a rifle as a toy. I want every man using that rifle to kill.

NO ONE IS THINKING IF EVERYONE
IS THINKING ALIKE

It was not necessary for staff officers to agree with Gen. Patton. He followed Ben Franklin's idea that no one was thinking if everyone was thinking alike. Gen. Patton did not want staff officers to follow his every whim. He was harsh with officers who would differ and not have any valid reason for the difference of opinion about a mission or problem.

One morning a newly commissioned National Guard Colonel objected to a training plan which our staff had prepared. Many of these new colonels received their military rank by political appointment and not for military merit. Gen. Patton was patient and asked of the colonel, "List your reasons for objecting to this training plan."

"I just do not think it will work!" The colonel wanted to appear important more than he wanted to object to the plan.

"Why?" The colonel had not learned a storm was brewing when Gen. Patton used the word, "Why."

"That training plan is too ambitious with too little time," the colonel was not losing any of his arrogance.

"Why?" Gen. Patton asked again. "Give reasons. This command will not play hunches! All of our plans are too ambitious! I always want more than one hundred per cent out of every man. Give me reasons! War is too dangerous to make decisions which are not based on sound facts. Give me your reasons for objecting to this plan!"

"I just do not think it will work!" The colonel insisted.

Gen. Patton went into his display of temper. "Now there is your problem, colonel! You just do not think! I will not have any non-thinkers on this staff. Wars are not won by non-thinkers and commanders making decisions on hunches."

The colonel did not respond. His arrogance was gone.

Gen. Patton continued, "We all have to be thinking every second. That is the reason for our deep breathing. We got to get all the oxygen we can into the brain. Battle plans must be based on facts - cold hard facts. If we do not get the facts, we cannot make good decisions. We will lose battles and men will be killed who should be permitted to live. Every officer and every man must think for himself and be thinking every second. I want my orders followed to the letter after we decide on a battle plan, but I do not want any man around me who "just does not think." We may have different ideas, but we will settle on a battle plan. When we settle on a plan, that is the plan we will use. Not because I order it but because it is the best plan based on cold hard facts. That is the whole idea of these frequent staff meetings. I want every last one of you to know the battle plan and know why it is the best."

Gen. Patton hesitated, "There is no place for any man in any war who does not think. Do you have any questions about this plan, colonel?"

"No, sir!"

"Is there anything you want to say about this plan?" Gen. Patton continued to spank the colonel. "No, sir!" All of his arrogance was gone.

I never saw the colonel again. I asked our Adjutant what happened to the colonel and was told he had been transferred.

I remember one staff meeting when I was on the spot for a decision which I had made as the Judge Advocate; the attorney for the command. I decided that we

SPECIAL LECTURE FOR ALL OFFICERS

FIRST CHAPEL SERVICE IN THE DESERT
GEN. PATTON IN FRONT ROW

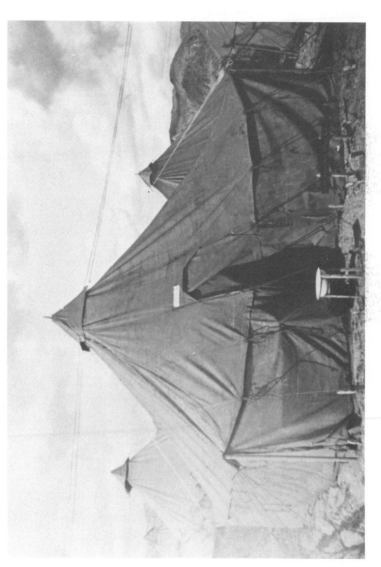

AUTHOR'S TENT WITH SOLAR HEATED WASH BASIN

LATRINE AT END OF OFFICERS' TENTS

SOURCE OF DRINKING WATER - THE LISTER BAG

EASY TO GET LOST IN THE DESERT

DESERT BUGLER READY TO GIVE THE EVENING SIGNAL

EVERY EVENING A FORMATION FOR LOWERING OF THE FLAG

should court-martial one of our regular army majors who had been involved in an auto accident on the road between Palm Springs and Indio, California. The major had caused an auto accident because he was driving too drunk to walk. At the scene of the accident, the major had been abusive and profane to the ladies in the car which the major's car had struck. In addition, the major had insulted the arresting officers of California. These state officers took all of the major's abuse and returned him to our military police although they, the California officers, had every legal right to put him in jail in Palm Springs or Indio.

The following Monday morning, the major was sober and on duty with his troops. When the facts were given to me by our Military Police, I advised that the major had to be court-martialed for his criminal acts. My decision would result in the major being fined several hundred dollars, perhaps a jail sentence and dismissal from the military service.

I discussed my decision with our Chief of Staff. The charges were prepared and filed with our higher headquarters with a request for the formation of a general court-martial, our highest military court.

The feuding among the officers started immediately. There were many who argued for the major. It was only a few months after Pearl Harbor. We needed every officer we could get. The major was a West Point graduate, a trained officer. We needed officers with training. It was not a crime for soldiers to drink. I was under personal attack. The rank of Judge Advocate was supposed to be held by a full colonel. I was only a lieutenant. It was argued that I was too young and had been given too much authority. Also, it was said I did not know anything about military law and court-martial procedure despite my being

No One Is Thinking if Everyone
Is Thinking Alike

assigned to work with the court-martial courts for over a year. In addition when called to active duty, I was the attorney for the State of Indiana for one of the larger counties. All of my arguments were sound; however, the court-martial papers were returned from higher headquarters with an instruction to reprimand the major, give him a reduction in pay, and permit him to continue in command of the troops. I was not gaining any friends on the staff.

Gen. Patton reviewed the case at a staff meeting. I remember his closing words, "Lieutenant, you decision has put us in an embarrassing position with our higher headquarters. Do you have any explanation for your decision?"

I started to answer from the back of the room. Gen. Patton stopped me, saying, "Get on up here, Lieutenant, so you can be seen and heard."

I walked to the front of the room and faced the high ranking officers on the front row, most of them West Point graduates. They were wearing their war faces. I attempted to speak slowly, "I agree with all of you that the major is a good officer. We all know him. The truth is he had an auto accident. He cannot deny the accident. He cannot deny being drunk. He was so drunk he could not stand without leaning on his car. He could not walk one step down the center line of the road as he was asked to do by the California officers. These officers returned him seventy miles to our camp. The major was delivered to our Military Police with our promise to the California officers that we would prosecute the major for driving while under the influence of liquor."

I was not gaining. The war faces never changed. I decided to answer Gen. Patton's question. "To answer the question about our command being embarrassed, it should never be embarrassing to follow our own military laws. We should not be embarrassed to keep the promise our military police made to the California police officers. If we had not made this promise, you can be sure that the major would be in jail in Palm Springs under prosecution by the law enforcement officers of California. I can understand the reasoning of our higher headquarters. We do need trained officers."

I was not gaining. I attacked the "front line" staff members with their stiff war faces. "Is there any one of you that would expect to get drunk, swear at ladies, strike at police officers, and expect to be given a light tap on your wrist? Would you expect to avoid being court-martialed because you were a trained officer? Is the conduct of the major that of an officer and a gentleman under the definition of our Articles of War? If any of you would expect to escape punishment for your military crimes, what kind of an example would this be for the men we command? Would this put us in an embarrassing position with our troops? If an enlisted man had caused such a serious accident could you believe that our high headquarters would not insist that the soldier be court-martialed? Would this help Gen. Patton's command to permit such military and civilian crimes to go without the punishment demanded by our Army Regulations?"

I looked at Gen. Patton who was standing at the window in the wall at the side of our staff briefing room. I looked to him for support, but I could not see any change in the expression on his face.

We called the opening in the side of our building a "window," but it did not have any glass nor screen. Half of the side of the room could be raised on a hinge to let the heat out of the building.

I decided to end my argument with some of Gen. Patton's own words, "Gen. Patton has said so many times that we must train here as if we were in combat. We must try to keep our training as close to war-like conditions as possible. We must always work as if we were in actual combat with the enemy. Any officer who cannot control his drinking in California could not control his drinking in combat." I could not see any eyes nor heads moving in agreement.

I hesitated for support but none came. "Gentlemen, I want to take this opportunity to answer some of the personal attacks which some of you have made on me. Some of you have said that I should be court-martialed." Again I looked at Gen. Patton and expected him to stop me. He was looking out the window into the desert.

Getting angry, I let my anger show. "I am not on trial in this case. I would be on trial if I had failed to follow the Regulations for the office of the Judge Advocate. None of us should expect to avoid court-martial if we failed to perform our duty. To those who argue that I have been too hard on our friend, the major, I can file additional charges. There is evidence the major revealed military secrets in Palm Springs. It is reported he told a bartender the day our payroll leaves Indio. It takes several hundred thousand dollars to pay all of our soldiers. I prepared only one charge with the hope that the punishment would not keep our friend from further military service. I could prepare several criminal charges against our friend. Embarrassed? How embarrassed would this command be if I had prepared several charges. I know that I am young, as some of you have charged. However, I am the only attorney on the staff. It is not a pleasant task to file criminal charges against a fellow officer. How embarrassed would this command be if I had not prepared the court-martial charge against the major? Gen. Patton, I will answer any questions you might have."

I looked at Gen. Patton who stepped towards to me and asked the staff, "Any of you want to ask Lieutenant Williamson any questions?"

No one said a word. Gen. Patton said, "You answered my questions, Lieutenant."

I walked to the back of the room. Gen. Patton did not say anything for several seconds. His eyes attempted to meet the eyes of every officer in the room. I was beginning to fear he would dismiss the meeting without taking any position on the court-martial charges and dismiss me from the assignment as Judge Advocate.

Gen. Patton said, "Lieutenant, you are exactly right. Our higher headquarters is wrong. They do not have to lead any troops into combat! We have to live with the troops and California. You write a nasty letter to our higher headquarters. Put in the letter the words you have given us. Keep it short. Do not argue with them. Just tell them the major will be court-martialed. Get that answer on my desk by noon. I'll sign it and get it back to headquarters."

When I returned to my desk and work as Assistant to Col. Gay, the Corps G-4, he said, "You presented that quite well. One thing I am sure, we both prefer to make property decisions rather than people decisions. Gen. Patton never likes to oppose higher headquarters, but he will if the troops are involved."

"What is your guess on what higher headquarters will do on Gen. Patton's answer?"

No One Is Thinking if Everyone
Is Thinking Alike

"They will transfer the major to some other higher headquarters. They always do. That's the reason so many in higher headquarters don't know much about commanding troops."

I never heard what happened to the court-martial charges. The major was transferred - to a higher headquarters!

KNOW WHAT YOU KNOW AND KNOW
WHAT YOU DO NOT KNOW

"How do we know that?" was a frequent question asked by Gen. Patton. Now and then the answer would be, "That information came from Washington!"

With such an answer, Gen. Patton would go into one of his short lectures, saying, "Washington is the most unreliable source of information you could ever use! An officer in a swivel chair in the Pentagon actually knows nothing. All that he knows comes from soldiers in the field. I do not want to come down too hard on these poor souls in the Pentagon, but they know almost nothing from first hand knowledge. Everything they know is second-hand information. All they do is collect paper facts from the field organizations."

Gen. Patton instructed, "We must always know exactly what we know and what we do not know. Never get the two confused! If we get confused over what we know we can cause many men to die. That is the problem of having our Army controlled from Washington. The officers in the Pentagon seldom get near the fighting to see exactly what goes on in war."

Gen. Patton demanded that we sort through our known and unknown facts to know exactly what we really knew. It could be a shipment of new tanks from Detroit. Some officer might say that the tanks were shipped on a certain date because the shipping notice said when they were shipped. Gen. Patton would explain, "That is the paper work on the tanks which some clerk in some office typed. That clerk would not know for sure that the tanks were even loaded on the flat cars! Or they could be loaded and still sitting in some rail yard waiting to be hooked onto a train."

159

Know What You Know and Know
What You Do Not Know

If no one knew where the tanks were, Gen. Patton would assign one of us to get on the telephone and follow-up on the tanks every day. Often his briefing would end, "Raise hell if there is any foul-up!"

This type of management saved thousands of hours in staff meetings. No time was wasted on what someone had told us about our equipment. We had to go out and try the equipment in the field.   We read all of the technical manuals but did not accept any of the information as facts until the facts were proven by actual "desert-sand" experience.

Gen. Patton lectured, "Every tank and every truck is as different as every man. Make sure every driver knows his tank or truck.   He must know exactly how many gallons of gas and oil are needed for a mile and for an hour - and at different speeds and conditions. Check the tank every time it is refueled. If it is using too much of anything, send it to heavy maintenance. We must know our equipment."

Our staff played a little game with Washington, all done with Gen. Patton's instruction!   Washington was trying to help every unit as much as possible by sending experts to us from the manufacturers of our tanks and trucks.

Many of these experts were of draft age and could be called to active duty with the Army.   Washington wanted us to have a dozen or more of these experts with us all of the time. Gen. Patton did not want anyone in his organization who was not under his total and complete command. We seldom used any of the experts more than one day. We were instructed to get all of the information we could from the expert including his full name, address, and draft number! At the end of the day, Gen. Patton

would see the expert in his office and tell him not to return
unless he was in uniform. I remember the shock of some
of these experts when Gen. Patton would smile and say,
"We appreciate your coming to visit us. We need all of
the help we can get. We want you here with us full time!
We have your name and address so I am writing to your
draft board asking for you personally to come serve with
us."

Most of the experts were under forty years of age.
Some of them would protest and explain that they were
excused from the draft because they were necessary to help
industry. Gen. Patton would say, "I have hundreds of men
who could be excused from the draft! Most of the soldiers
had civilian salaries higher then they are now paid in the
Army. If I were running Washington all of you would
make the same wage as soldiers in the Army!"

I am not sure any of the experts Gen. Patton asked
to have drafted ever returned to the desert. We had our
own experts! I remember a "visiting expert" who became
angry when one of our second lieutenants was reading a
newspaper during the expert's lecture.

The visiting expert asked our second lieutenant, "I
suppose you know more about this front-wheel drive jeep
than I do!"

The lieutenant did not put down his paper as he
answered, "I would hope so!"

"Then you should be up here giving this lecture!
What is your name? I am going to report you to Gen.
Patton!"

The lieutenant continued to read the paper as he
said, "My name is down in the left-hand corner of the
diagram you are using. My company made all of the blue
prints for your company. Report me to Gen. Patton if you

wish. I know that most of the men in this class know as much about the transmission on that truck as you do because I've told them! When you see Gen. Patton, he will tell you he will be writing to your draft board to have you drafted into military service."

The visiting expert gave us a recess and never returned from the recess! When we told Gen. Patton of our "absent" expert, he laughed.

Gen. Patton resented Washington paying high consulting fees on a per day basis to the civilian experts "to spend a few days" with the Army. He wanted "full time" experts in the Army. He did not want civilians drawing high salaries working every day with soldiers. A great number of soldiers and officers could have avoided the draft and remained in civilian life on higher salaries.

Gen. Patton often explained the problems of being in Washington, "Now where would an arm-chair expert in Washington get his facts on the use of a tank in the field? From the company that manufactured the tank! Now what will the manufacturer say about his tank? He is sure to cut the fuel to the bare minimum to make his tank look good. This information is sent to the supply sergeant in Washington who adds all of this into a fancy chart. Of course, the sergeant will add twenty percent to the figure to make sure there is no shortage of gas. This goes to the lieutenant who adds a bit more to make sure that he cannot be blamed for a tank being out of gas. Keep passing such figures up the chain of command, and you may have twice as much gas as you need. We have to know every piece of our equipment!"

Gen. Patton advised, "Wars are won by knowing what we know. We must know exactly what we need for every day. If we try to carry into combat more gas, oil, supply parts, or anything that we do not need, it could lose a war as quickly as letting a soldier carry a pound more than he needs on his back. We must cut to the bone because we are going to travel fast!"

One day our gas supplies were low for all of the Desert Training Command. We could plan for only a one day maneuver. One lieutenant filled all of his tanks to the top. When he was questioned about taking on so much gas, he answered, "The Army Tech Manual from Washington says the gas tanks must be filled to the top at all times to prevent moisture accumulating in the tank and causing rust."

When Gen. Patton learned that several tanks were missing because of lack of gas there was an explosion - by Gen. Patton. He scolded, "No damn gas tank will ever rust out before this war is over! How much moisture is there in the desert? Almost none! Forget about rust in the tanks. We will be moving so fast that rust will never catch us. Know exactly what every tank needs for the maneuver. Ration the gas with a definite reserve, but don't fill'er up as if you were pulling into an auto service station. We are trying to learn how to run these tanks to kill enemy soldiers. We are not in this war to prevent rust in the tanks."

In a sober mood, Gen. Patton explained to the tank drivers, "You must know your tank and how much fuel it uses. When you know, you will not be worried about having too little gas."

Several times Gen. Patton told a story about how to lose a war. With his boyish grin, he related a story of a maneuver in Louisiana. "Relax for a few minutes, and I will tell you how to lose a war. Wars are won by little things; often at unimportant crossroads. Last year in

Know What You Know and Know
What You Do Not Know

Louisiana, 1941, we had a Chinese national enlisted in our American Army. He looked like any other American soldier in his uniform except he did not understand much English and could speak almost no English. Well, this poor soldier got lost on one of our maneuvers. Being unable to speak English he could not ask where his outfit was camped. I doubt that he could pronounce the name of his outfit so that any American could understand him. Being in the American uniform and walking along the highway, civilian drivers gave him a ride until the Chinese soldier would point to the door indicating he wanted out. This poor soldier was stranded at last at a crossroad where he attempted to hitchhike a ride with any Army vehicle of any unit.

The big problem with this soldier was that he did not know exactly how to hitchhike. He used his index finger to point forward instead of using his thumb to point in the direction he wanted a ride. Can you guess what happened? For one convoy of Army trucks the Chinese soldier sent the entire convoy down the road the Chinese soldier pointed. Of course, no driver stopped since the man did not act like a hitchhiker. He was directing traffic!"

Gen. Patton paused, "Do all of you realize how easy it would be for one enemy soldier in an American uniform to destroy our firing capability? This story does not get any better. Half a dozen officers stopped and tried to tell this Chinese soldier how to direct traffic. They gave up when they could not get him to understand English. These officers did not know enough to know that the soldier was wanting a ride and did not want to direct traffic. This soldier knew more than all of the officers! He knew he was lost! That man deserves a medal for teaching us how to lose wars. Always know where your outfit is going. If you do not know, say so and find out. Would you believe it took us a week to locate all of the troops this Chinese soldier sent in the wrong directions. He scattered troops, trucks, and tanks all over Louisiana and Texas!"

Several times Gen. Patton mentioned this Chinese soldier in the evening meetings in his tent. I remember his stressing, "So many people in this world are as confused as that Chinese hitchhiker who pointed with his index finger instead of his thumb. How many can put into words exactly what they know and what they want out of life. We get a ride here and take a trip there, but we never really know where we are going. We live our lives like the Chinese hitchhiker."

One evening Gen. Patton was telling this story when one of our highest ranking colonels confessed, "General, your pearls of wisdom hit me harder than all the rest. I am the SOB that gave that Chinese solder his military police armband so the troops would know he was directing traffic! I have never had the guts to admit this. I tried to talk to that soldier and all he would say was, 'No-eat, no-eat!' I pointed northeast. So he pointed northeast for the next convoy of trucks. We sent some units into enemy areas. It was long after this happened that it came to me that this soldier was not saying 'northeast' but was trying to say he was hungry!"

We laughed. Gen. Patton said, "I should keep you from getting your star as a brigadier general!" The colonel replied, "You would have every right to block my promotion. But I can tell you one thing, in training or in combat, I am going to check every MP at every crossroad. Better we should hold the convoys in position than scatter troops all over the battle area.

This colonel finished the war with the three stars of a Lieutenant General. He was G4 for the Third Army for all of the drives through to Berlin. It was not an easy task to keep all of Gen. Patton's troops with fuel, food and clothing - including white socks every day for every soldier.

GET UP FRONT!

One of Gen. Patton's orders was "Get up front!" The civilian rule would be "Get on site." His orders often aroused laughter. "I want every member of this staff to get up front at least once every day. You will never know what is going on unless you can hear the whistle and whine of the bullets. You must lead the men. It is easier to lead than to push."

He would be silent for several seconds before saying with a big smile, "Besides, having you senior colonels up front is a great incentive and temptation for the younger officers. Nothing like creating a vacancy to get a promotion!"

We laughed with him. He had made his point. He wanted every officer, staff and line command, to "serve" the troops so completely that no soldier would ever think of shooting any one other than the enemy. No officer had to be in any fear of being shot by his own troops. Hatred for poor officers could exceed the hatred for the enemy. Gen. Patton insisted on the type of leadership which would not be in fear of being in front of the troops.

Some writers have said that Gen. Patton was hated by his troops. This is totally false. Gen. Patton was on the front lines often enough that many of his men could have used a stray bullet to express their hatred. My suspicion is that many German soldiers had chances to shoot Gen. Patton. I am sure that many German soldiers saw his shining helmet at the front. Gen. Patton's troops respected him so much, that any German soldier with an ounce of sense would have been afraid to shoot Gen. Patton. The Germans knew that if Gen. Patton was shot by the Germans, the American troops would be so enraged that no German prisoners would be taken alive for weeks.

The Germans also knew that when they faced Gen. Patton there was a good chance that they would be captured.

Gen. Patton used the old log chain idea, saying, "Trying to lead men from behind makes you a driver and not a leader. It is easier to lead men just as it is easier to pull a log chain. You cannot push a log chain and you cannot push troops. The troops will keep running back to you for instructions - really from fear. A leader has to be ahead of his men. You got to know what is going on all the time. You cannot swim without being in the water! You cannot ice skate without being on ice. No one ever learned to skate on a map board. Take the map with you and get up front!"

There is a story about Gen. Patton which I have learned is not fiction. Gen. Patton returned to his headquarters from the front lines to find his engineers poring over maps trying to decide where to cross a river. Gen. Patton advised, "Cross the river at this point."
He pointed to a spot on the map and marked the spot with a red marker.

A senior colonel said, "General, we have little information about the depth of the river where you pointed. We would probably have to build a pontoon bridge, and we do not know the soil conditions of the banks."

"We will cross where I made the mark! Every man can walk across, and I am certain the tanks can get enough solid ground to drive across. The banks are solid. The river is wide but quite shallow."

"How can we be sure, General?"
"Take a look at my pants! That's how shallow the water is. I walked across without collecting any enemy fire!"

Often I am asked why Gen. Patton was so crude as to urinate in the Rhine river when he crossed into Germany with his Third Army. He said so many times that he intended to do what "every great military leader, such as Caesar and Napoleon had done when they crossed the Rhine; urinate in the Rhine to show no fear of the attacking the mainland of Germany!"

Gen. Patton would not break tradition with the great military commanders of history!

NEVER MAKE A DECISION
TOO EARLY OR TOO LATE

Frequently some new staff officer would want to make definite decisions about some training plan which had been received from higher headquarters.

Gen. Patton would be patient and ask, "Colonel, when is this plan supposed to be completed."

"I'm not sure, General."

"Until we know exactly what is required, let's confine our decisions to the training we know we must complete. We have enough to do without trying to anticipate everything that comes out of Washington." Gen. Patton paused, "Besides, chances are Washington will issue a dozen revisions before they give us their final plan."

"We should have a standard operating procedure. That's the way we did it when I was in the Pentagon!"

"Colonel, we are not in the Pentagon. It is a good idea to have guidelines for making decisions, but in war nothing is standard. The Pentagon can make standard operating decisions for all situations because all of their situations can be made standard. Combat decisions are never standard!"

At other times he said, "There is a right time to make every decision. Trying to find the right time is the most important factor for all decisions. It is a mistake to make a decision too early, and it is a mistake to make a decision too late. The biggest mistake is to never make a decision!" Gen. Patton would pause and smile, "Every old maid agrees with me!"

"The best policy is to delay the decision as long as possible so that more facts can be collected. When the decision has to be made we will never hesitate. Making a decision too early will result in making too many changes.

Never Make A Decision
Too Early Or Too Late

Making decisions too late always results in emergency decision making - pressure decisions. We do not want to create any emergency situations which the enemy might use against us. If we plan carefully, we will never have any emergency decisions to make."

This was in 1942 or about twenty years before the management experts invented the new decision making process called, "PERT," for Program Evaluation and Review Techniques. In 1942, Gen. Patton perfected this process with his own four letter words!

I can imagine what Gen. Patton would say about the new invention of management; namely, "MBO" Management By Objectives. He would explode, "What in hell were the experts doing before they had objectives? Did they try to run a corporation with no objective except to keep the coffee pot hot? That's like trying to sail a boat without a rudder! Without knowing the mission, no one knows where they are going. Every soldier must know our objectives at all times."

Gen. Patton was giving the MBO lectures before the letters were invented. He was always stressing, "No man can do anything without knowing what he is doing. Let the American soldier know what he is fighting for and why. When we let him know what has to be done, he will do it! No soldier in the world can match the Americans for getting the job done. Generals and staff officers do not win wars! Soldiers win wars! The soldier must know what he is doing at all times. He must know the objective!"

The mission or objective was all important and had to be obtained at any cost in property or lives. Gen. Patton warned us, "There is nothing wrong with retreating from the fighting at the front!" He would pause without smiling, "But you had damn well better be on a litter and coming back feet first! I will shoot any man I see turning his back on the enemy unless he has been shot. I got a medal in World War I for saying I would shoot any man who deserted!"

Gen. Patton never delayed in making a decision when it was time to make it. He cautioned, "When a decision has to be made, make it. There is no totally right time for anything."

Several months after the first edition of this book was published I received a letter from a staff officer serving with an embassy in a foreign country. He asked a simple question, "Did Gen. Patton make his staff make the decisions, or did Gen. Patton make the decisions? Our Commanding General makes us make every decision. He has not made a decision since I have been here! If the decision is correct, he takes the credit. If it is wrong, we get the blame!"

It was an easy letter to answer. It was obvious this general was so afraid of making a wrong decision that he never made any decisions. Gen. Patton made every major decision. The blame and credit was reversed on Gen. Patton's staff from that of the embassy general. If the decision was good, Gen. Patton would give credit to the staff member. If the decision was wrong, Gen. Patton would quip, "I goofed on that I should have caught it. I should have caught it." Often he would explain, "We did not spend enough time getting the facts on this problem."

Major commands issue orders over a signature indicating, "By Order of the Commanding General" with the name of the organization. Gen. Patton's name went on every order and he accepted full responsibility for every decision.

TOO MUCH IF'N, PERHAPS'N AND MAYBE'N
WILL NEVER WIN A BATTLE

Gen. Patton demanded that the staff exert every effort to get all of the facts before making a decision. In addition he put a limit on the amount of time we had to collect the facts. When the hour of decision arrived, there was no delay nor hesitation.

He used simple sentences to impress upon us what we had to do. He would say, "This decision may prove to be something other than the best, but we will do what has to be done. We will go with what we got!"

When we received orders from Washington, Gen. Patton might protest and argue over what we considered an improper order. When the final word was received he would say, "Whether we like it or not, this is the way it is going to be. We will go with it."

I remember a colonel from a National Guard unit that Gen. Patton "retired" without any perhaps'n or maybe'n. I had been searching the Army regulations trying to get the laws on what could be done with a National Guard colonel. I was sure that National Guard colonels came under all of our Army Regulations, but I wanted to see it in a law book. The problem was given to me by the commander of our Military Police company.

This National Guard colonel was a newly commissioned politically-appointed officer who would go to war, but he wanted to go in style. He wanted all of the privileges of the high rank without any inconvenience. The facts given to me were that the colonel spent his nights in an air- conditioned motel in Indio, California. He spent his days in an air conditioned trailer parked outside of our maneuver areas. I checked with the staff officers of the National Guard about their commander living in air

Too Much If'n, Perhaps'n, and Maybe'n
Will Never Win a Battle

conditioned quarters. They confirmed the facts. They confessed their governor had appointed a political friend who did not have any military experience. This was not unusual in World War II. Everyone wanted to be a colonel!

The National Guard unit attempted to comply with all of their colonel's orders. They maintained his air conditioned trailer in the desert, far from our headquarters. The air conditioner was run by a military generator. They took rations (food) to the woman in the trailer thinking it was the colonel's wife.

According to the officers, no one objected to taking rations to this attractive young woman. The soldiers seldom saw women in the desert! None of the staff objected to visiting the colonel's trailer! During the heat of the desert sun, the colonel spent all of his time in the trailer. At night the colonel drove to Indio and spent the night with another woman. No one knew which woman, if either, was his wife!

The colonel told his staff he wanted a quart of milk and a morning paper on the step of his trailer every morning. He had to leave Indio before the Los Angeles papers arrived. The milk had to be iced, and the paper had to be picked up in Indio by one of the trucks that drove to Indio for rations.

I was given all of the facts from the Military Police. It was hot in the desert, but our only air-conditioned room was in our make-shift field hospital. Gen. Patton's tent was as hot as any of the tents for the troops. When the Captain of the Military Police traced the man to the trailer in the desert, the Captain came to me for advice. He was fearful for the safety of the woman living alone in the trailer at night.

Too Much If'n, Perhaps'n, and Maybe'n
Will Never Win a Battle

I advised the Captain that the only charge that could be filed against the colonel was the broad catch-all charge of "conduct unbecoming an officer and a gentleman." We could have suspicions that the colonel was having intercourse with both of his women, but the proof had to come from the women. This would be difficult to prove if both women were "well cared for."

Gen. Patton had never issued an order that every man live in the desert. This was expected without an order! However, I could not make a case of disobeying an order without an order. National Guard officers were appointed and commissioned by the governors of the states. National Guard troops came under federal control when called to active military duty by the President. This National Guard unit was on active duty with their own trucks and motor equipment. Their equipment records were not on our property lists. I discussed the problem with our Chief of Staff. Before we could decide on a definite plan, a battalion commander asked Gen. Patton if he could get an air-conditioned trailer for his headquarters and bring his wife to camp.

Gen. Patton's prompt retort was, "Hell no!"

"Then how does that National Guard colonel get to keep his wife in that trailer about twenty miles from here near the base of the Chocolate Mountains?"

Since the trailer was outside of our maneuver area, Gen. Patton had never spotted the trailer.

Our Chief of Staff reported the facts which we had on the problem.

When the Chief of Staff finished, Gen. Patton ordered, "Williamson, you are our Judge Advocate. Get that SOB court-martialled!"

I had to reply, "General, we have never published

an order that everyone must live in the desert without air-conditioning. We cannot charge him with disobeying a direct order. The only charge I could file would be under "conduct unbecoming an officer and a gentleman."

Some officer in the back of the room whispered, "I would say this SOB is becoming quite a man!" Gen. Patton did not laugh if he heard the loud whisper.

The Chief of Staff cautioned, "These National Guard colonels are a problem since they have political ties with the governors who have great influence in Washington."

Gen. Patton asked, "Williamson, you were in public office as a civilian. What do you say about this colonel?"

It was an easy question to answer, "That colonel with his trailer is closer to the highway than we are. He is sure to be discovered by some reporter. We would have more problems with the newspapers than with any political influence in Washington."

Gen. Patton asked of the staff, "How sure are we of the facts? Could it be this woman in the desert is his sister, and the trailer belongs to his sister? This newspaper and milk delivery stuff sounds more like latrine rumor than truth. What facts do we actually know?"

The Military Police captain answered, "General, we know that this man spends his nights in Indio with one woman and his days in this air-conditioned trailer with another woman. He has never been in the desert with his own troops. All of this we know. We do not know what his relationship is with these two women."

"Williamson, how about unauthorized use of an Army vehicle?" Gen. Patton asked of me.

"This National Guard unit came to us with its own equipment. We have not had the time to inventory the equipment and assume control over all of their property. This colonel can do anything he wants with his own staff car. I doubt that I could make a good case against him on such a charge."

Gen. Patton asked me directly, "What trouble could we get into if we haul that trailer and woman hauled into Indio?"

I had to make a quick decision, "No great amount of trouble since the trailer is on federal land without any permit of any kind. We could get into trouble if we had an auto accident on the highway to Indio. No one should ride in the trailer when it is pulled out of the desert nor on the highway."

"Gen. Patton did not delay in making a decision, "I am going to retire that SOB from the United States Army. Captain, take one of your military police vehicles and hook onto that trailer. Put the gal in one of our ambulances along with the colonel. Put two police cars in front and back of the trailer with their red lights flashing and sirens on. This should prevent any accident. We will take the colonel and his "sister" into town in the style to which they have been living - with red lights! Put both of them in the ambulance. Do not exceed forty miles per hour."

"What shall I tell the colonel?" the Captain asked.

"Don't tell him anything! I am going to be with you. I want to take care of that SOB myself! When I get through with him he may have to retire from the National Guard for physical disability!"

There was no if'n or maybe'n about Gen. Patton's decision. He did what had to be done. Such quick decisions were not the usual rule with the politically appointed National Guard officers. Under different commands many such officers went on maneuvers with

Too Much If'n, Perhaps'n, and Maybe'n
Will Never Win a Battle

fancy air- conditioned trailers and with their wives. I remember the staff discussions about such conduct in other commands. The discussions usually ended with the words, "If this gets too bad, we may have to take some action."

Gen. Patton did not delay. It was interesting when some new officer would suggest, "This does not seem to be the right time to . . .." Gen. Patton would break in, "There is no perfect time for anything. We will do what has to be done, and we will do it now!"

After Gen. Patton finished with his attack on the National Guard colonel, we heard the colonel decided to retire from military service. We never received a protest from either wife, the governor of the state, nor any politician in Washington.

Gen. Patton's daughter gave me a quote from her father; "Prompt action immediately on a wrong decision may be far better than the right decision made days later."

NO GOOD DECISION WAS EVER MADE
IN A SWIVEL CHAIR

Our staff meetings would last an hour if some staff officer would say, "Our decision on this matter is based on the assumption that . . ."

"Whoa! Hold up!" Gen. Patton would interrupt, "We do not ever want to assume anything. Why is it we cannot get the facts?"

If the officer could give a valid explanation, Gen. Patton would be satisfied. If not, it would be a day the officer would never forget. Constantly Gen. Patton preached the "get the facts" theme. He stressed, "We must always have all of the facts. A decision without all of the facts is no decision at all. No good decision was ever made in a swivel chair."

We laughed, but Gen. Patton did not smile. He continued, "I mean it! No good decision was ever made in a swivel chair. Better to have a decision made on horseback than in a swivel chair. A man in a swivel chair does not have his body juices going to the right places. Nothing is going to his brain after twenty minutes of his swiveling around in a soft chair. All of our brains will be in our shoes in twenty minutes! We must get out of our swivel chairs and know exactly what is going on!"

One day a colonel was under attack by Gen. Patton for a decision based on the weather. The colonel explained, "General, we cannot predict the weather. We must assume average weather conditions and plan accordingly."

"We never assume anything is average," G e n . Patton said. "If we do any assuming, we will assume the worst weather."

The colonel tried to argue, "We might wait a day

before we launch the maneuver."

"Then why make a decision now. Have you contacted the 'weather makers' - the men who tell us what is going to happen to our weather? What do they say?"

"I did not contact the weather section. I just assumed average weather."

Gen. Patton scolded, "We will have men's lives hanging on our decisions! We cannot assume anything. Whether we are in the desert or in actual combat, we must get the facts. How are we going to feel when we make a decision and several hundred men are killed? Want to try assuming they are not dead? Never forget, colonel, the life you save could be your own."

Gen. Patton wanted exact facts about everything pertaining to a maneuver. He wanted us to know the exact quantity of fuel in the tanks - hot and cold! He wanted to know in seconds the number of gallons of gas needed for a division to move a mile - thirty miles or any number he asked. He wanted the exact weight of rations a soldier had to carry should the field kitchens not be able to keep up with an advance.

So often he concluded a staff lecture with the words, "Let's never have to look at each other and say, 'If only we had known!' We want to always know."

One time we did not give Gen. Patton all of the facts. If the Jap Navy had changed course in the Pacific there would have been an amazing change in the history of World War II. In the summer of 1942, the Jap Navy had a large invasion force in the Pacific. Mexico had just declared war on Japan. When our G-2, Intelligence Officer, reported this Jap task force in the Pacific, Gen. Patton put every man into high gear to defend the Lower California Bay of Mexico.

No Good Decision Was Ever Made
In A Swivel Chair

Gen. Patton ordered, "The Japs will land in this bay in Mexico. Mexico will not be able to stop any invasion. The beaches of this Lower California Bay are superior for landing a large invasion force. Several hundred thousand men could be landed on the beaches in this area! It will be easy to run through Mexico. Los Angeles is only a short distance from Mexico. Orange County and Los Angeles produce most of our aircraft. Any fool knows this would be the best objective for the Japs. If they knock out our aircraft production and get a force into Los Angeles, we are in for a long war. We will prepare to meet the bastards on the beaches of Mexico!"

Our excitement did not decrease when the Jap force appeared to be heading for Alaska.

"Alaska is not the objective!" Gen. Patton insisted. "This is to throw us off. They will never land in Alaska. No war has ever been fought so close to the Arctic Circle! The devils will hit Mexico!"

We collected all of the facts on Mexico. We knew the roads, the railroads, beaches, soil conditions, number of people in the towns - we had the facts! One major fact was not given to Gen. Patton; the amount of ammunition for our large guns. All of the ammunition for the tanks and field artillery had been fired during the desert maneuvers. No more ammunition was to be shipped for two weeks.

Our Desert Training Center was less than a hundred miles from the northern tip of the California Bay. We were in such a tight alert that no man slept in a bedding roll. Every one of us slept in uniform. We used our helmets for our pillows. If we had received orders from Washington as Gen. Patton expected, we would have been moving in less than sixty seconds. Gen. Patton wanted us

181

to cover that distance to Mexico in less than three hours.

We slept in our uniforms for three nights before Washington reported that the Japs had landed on the tip of the islands of Alaska.

We congratulated our Ordinance chief, "You can relax now and stop worrying about the ammunition for our tanks and field artillery."

All of the ammunition we had was for our small arms, the automatic pistols. If the Japs had struck Mexico, it would have been an interesting battle.

I am sure if Gen. Patton had learned of our ammunition shortage, it would not have changed his decision to attack the enemy. He would have said, "We will scare the hell out of them until Washington can fly in the ammunition!"

I am sure we would have raced our few tanks up and down the beaches with sirens screaming and dodging behind the sand hills so that the enemy could count the same tank dozens of times. We would have stirred up so much dust no sane enemy commander would chance trying to land against such a superior force!

By the time the Japs learned that our tanks could not fire, we would have been supplied by Washington.

When we held our first staff meeting after our Mexican alert, Gen. Patton said, "And I sat in my damn swivel chair and thought we were ready to fight! I made my decision without knowing all of the facts! I would still have moved down there. We could throw sand in their eyes!"

THE WAY TO WIN IS TO NEVER LOSE!

"We will win because we will never lose!" Gen. Patton explained to the troops. "War is the greatest game of life! Most games are played for a certain length of time like four quarters of football or nine innings of baseball. Not so with war. We will fight until we win. We will never give in." Gen. Patton's logic was so simple every man understood the message. Gen. Patton would not lose!

He explained in more detail, "There can never be defeat if a man refuses to accept defeat. Wars are lost in the mind before they are lost on the ground. No nation was ever defeated until the people were willing to accept defeat. England is defeated. The only hope is that Churchill is refusing to accept defeat.

When people are willing to give their lives for their country, the only way a nation can be defeated is to kill every man, woman, and child. In the history of the world this has never happened. Wars are lost in the minds of the people. We will never admit to the troops nor to the enemy that we will accept defeat."

"How did we win our first war?" Gen. Patton asked as he prepared to quote from the Declaration of Independence. We won the first war because the men signing the Declaration of Independence 'pledged their lives, their fortunes, and their sacred honor.' That Declaration was the declaration of war.

This idea of never losing matches Gen. Patton's principle that the body is never tired. It is the mind that thinks tiredness. The mind can eliminate the tiredness of the body.

This idea may seem new, but such ideas were mentioned in the Bible. As Gen. Patton explained, "There are several descriptions of death in the Bible, such as, 'He gave up the ghost.' Many patients in hospitals die when they give up and accept defeat. I recall a man in Michigan who built his own coffin. When the coffin was finished, the man died. I know several men who retired to build their dream homes. When they were finished, the men died. Man must have a battle in life if he is to live, but he will never be defeated if he will never give in to defeat."

Years later when I heard of the words of Churchill's famous school commencement address, I puzzled over who had this idea first, Gen. Patton or Churchill. Churchill's commencement address consisted of only nine words: "Never give in! Never give in! Never give in!" Not a single member of the graduating class would ever forget all of the words of the commencement speech!

Gen. Patton and Churchill met many times during the years of the first World War. Churchill was the first to design the tank. It is unimportant which man was the first to have the idea. This "never lose" thinking saved England from Hitler's invasion and helped Gen. Patton win many victories in World War II.

There are many examples of this simple idea in medical circles. The military amputation hospital staff often told the story of the high jumper who lost a leg but refused to stop high jumping. His mind controlled his body. On one leg he could jump higher than he ever jumped on two legs. He hopped towards the bar on one leg. It was the amputated leg which had always tripped the bar when he had two legs.

Patrick Henry had this idea in 1776 when he said, "Give me liberty or give me death!" When the mind refuses to give in, even unto death, there will always be a victory.

GEN. PATTON GREETING GEN. AND MRS. MARSHALL
ALWAYS THE AMERICAN FLAG WITH HONOR GUARD

SPECIAL MANEUVERS FOR GEN. MARHSALL AND STAFF
GEN. PATTON WILL NOT STAND IN THE SHADE

SOLDIERS LISTENING TO A GEN. PATTON LECTURE

SHIELD FOR BENEDICT ARNOLD AT WEST POINT

MONUMENT TO GEN. PATTON IN LUXEMBOURG

DECEMBER 21, 1945, DAY OF GEN. PATTON'S FUNERAL

GEN. PATTON'S SECOND GRAVE

GEN. PATTON'S FIRST GRAVE

NEVER LET THE ENEMY
PICK THE BATTLE SITE

Along with Gen. Patton's never-lose principle was the idea that we would always fight on our terms. "We will never let the enemy pick the battle site," Gen. Patton stressed, "Now and then we could get caught in a trap set by the enemy, but not if we are alert. We will always know more about what the enemy is going to do than their own commanders. The secret is to move fast and in a direction the enemy never expects. The chance of taking losses is too great to fight on a battle site which pleases the enemy. This causes the loss of lives of hundreds of fine American young men. We will decide where and when we will kill the enemy."

This idea is so simple it works! It is as simple as "never dig a foxhole." All of these make up the strategy of always attack, never defend.

The idea of picking the battle site is not new. It could be said that the idea started in the year 1215 when the people of England pointed their long spears at their king and demanded that he sign the Magna Charta. This gave the people the right to fight their legal battles in their own home towns. Prior to the Magna Charta the people had to fight their legal battles at any place the king decided would be best for him. This principle is followed in America. Cases must be tried in the venue (place) where the people live. This venue can be changed if it is impossible to get a fair trial in the home area.

This simple idea can work in business circles. Suppose you have a product to sell to an executive. Surround this executive with his secretary, telephone, and keep-things- the-same aides, and the sale of a new idea is impossible. All good selling- shots will be lost by a telephone call or an assistant who will argue against the sale. The best place to sell a new idea is at lunch or dinner at a "battle-site" selected by the salesman! The protective secretary and the no-change assistants are not there to fight for their old ideas.

Gen. Patton was specific not only about battle sites but also about enemies. He said, "You have to pick your enemies with as much care as you do your friends! Friends are great. Just wonderful to have. Friends are like wine - get better with years. But you need good enemies as much as you need good friends. Having the right enemies is more important than having the right friends. Get the right enemies, and you will have the right friends! You always know where your enemies are. Can never be sure about friends. Sad but true, only a few friends will always be loyal. These luke-warm friends cause people to say, 'Protect me from my friends; I can take care of my enemies!' God knows we have enough of these luke-warm friends in the service same as in civilian life. Try to get these types to stand for something. Make them put up or shut up. A great number of military officers I know have never stood for anything other than a short arm inspection! We can differ with each other and still be friends. You will not be my friend if you fail to level with me always."

Not all of these ideas were given by Gen. Patton at one briefing. He was constantly tossing in ideas, such as, "I have enemies, and I want them to stay enemies. They could never be a loyal friend to anything or anybody. I strike at them every chance I can get. It is far better to lose battles with true friends than to win with the enemy. You do not lose a battle when you fight with true friends because you will always be fighting again for the same things. There is no victory when you win with an enemy. That's the reason I have never liked politics and politicians. They are always switching sides - changing bed partners in their politics."

One morning Gen. Patton commented on how to treat friendly troops. "We dare not be too trusting of friendly troops whether they are our own or from some foreign country. We must not treat them as we do the enemy, but we must always wait and see how they fight under enemy fire. That is the acid test of a friend and of a soldier. No other military organization is going to fight as hard and as fast as we will fight. We must be prepared to find our flanks exposed because friendly troops will not move as fast as we will move. Until we know how friendly troops will fight, do not count on them to do much more than bring up our mail!"

One evening in his tent we were talking about enemies. Gen. Patton asked me about political friends since I had held public office when called to active duty. Gen. Patton gave me a quote which I have never forgotten. He had been reading the Bible before our discussion. He said he had just received a long letter from a friend. Col. Gay and Gen. Patton discussed this officer since both knew him. Then Gen. Patton said, "You know a true friend gives you a glimpse of God!"

These are the only words I ever heard Gen. Patton say which would support a belief in reincarnation.

NEVER FIGHT A BATTLE WHEN NOTHING
CAN BE GAINED BY WINNING

Gen. Patton explained, "So many battles are fought in war and in civilian life, and nothing is gained by the victory. Every battle we fight will result in a gain for us or we will not fight. We will never defend! We will always attack. In civilian life we fight over such unimportant things as what the weather will be or what it was ten years ago. There is no great gain in merely being right. To be right about some unimportant subject is not important."

Gen. Patton continued, "For example, nothing is gained by being right about who might be the best baseball or football player. Why waste time on fighting over such an unimportant battle. How many fights we could have avoided when we were kids if we had refused to fight unless we gained some advantage. I know! When we were young we got into fights for the fun of fighting! War is not fun. We are not going to fight any battles for fun!"

To support his preaching, Gen. Patton switched back and forth between war and civilian life. He advised, "Now every time we get close to the enemy we expect him to shoot at us. We want him to shoot! That way we can pinpoint exactly where the enemy is located. We will never go straight at the enemy if there is an easier way. We have the speed to move behind the enemy. It may be a bit scary behind enemy lines, but that is where wars are won. The natives behind the lines will not shoot much because they will not have anything to match our heavy guns. When we are behind the enemy, they will not shell us for fear they might hit some of their own troops. No soldier likes to fire into his own hometown and kinfolk. We will go in and take whatever we have to take to cut the enemy away from his supplies. We are self-contained. We have everything we need to stay behind enemy lines for days. We can capture any gasoline which we might need."

I remember Gen. Patton explaining why we would not be scared. He said, "We will not be scared because we know we can fight our way back to friendly troops any time we want. The best plan is to raise hell until the friendly troops can come to us. Nothing gains faster than success. When we get the enemy on the run, we will keep him running! Night and day we will drive and never stop. We will never rest when we are winning."

Gen. Patton paused frequently and looked at the troops to see if any officer wanted to ask a question. "We will keep driving whether we have anything to eat or not. We can always eat our shoes, our leather belts, or each other! We will operate as horse cavalry. We will 'graze' off of the captured land. We will capture food and gasoline from the enemy. Those poor devils will not have their own food! We will be eating it. We will teach the bastards that to surround us is to make sure they will die. When we are surrounded we can fire in any direction and hit the enemy."

This principle was expressed in the Battle of the Bulge when the American troops were surrounded. The Germans demanded surrender and the American commander responded with the famous word, "Nuts!" With support from the air and Gen. Patton's Third Army drive to the rescue, the Germans learned that nothing was gained by surrounding American troops. With Gen. Patton attacking, the Germans were always alarmed. They were always in fear of where he might attack!

Gen. Patton often supported his ideas with quotations from the Bible. Often the quotation would fit

189

Never Fight A Battle When Nothing
Can Be Gained By Winning

his remarks, but sometimes the quote would miss the mark.

I remember his quoting, "Never cast your pearls among swine!"

It would be difficult to see how this would fit any of his principles until he added, "If the battle is worth it, we will go in and win. If not, we are not going to get shot at without a reason. The Bible tells us not to waste our best on pigs. We are not going into any pig shoot-out! We will kill the enemy where he can be killed easily with the least amount of risk to us. We will not fight the battle the enemy wants us to fight. We will fight on our terms, and we will win always."

He usually finished with his theory, "You see, when we take on their best troops and knock the hell out of them, the others will throw down their guns and quit. They know we have only one thing in mind and that is to kill everyone of the bastards. Their leaders know that these damn pistols on my hips are going to kill the devils. We understand this business of war, and the enemy knows it. When they know they are going to be killed, they will quit before the fight starts."

Gen. Patton's theory was correct. Photos from World War II show thousands of Germans troops stacking their rifles and surrendering when there were no American troops to accept the surrender.

SUCCESS IS HOW YOU
BOUNCE ON THE BOTTOM

"In our great Country, most any fool can be a success at something. Look at the flagpole climbers and goldfish eaters! The problem with success is that it leads to failure. When you are on top there is no place to go but down."

This type of thinking was given by Gen. Patton in the smaller staff meetings. He enjoyed throwing out ideas for conversation. As he enjoyed reading the Bible, he enjoyed putting ideas into words.

"Life is like a roller-coaster. Life has its ups and downs. I've been up and down many times. Every time I get an award or win a victory, I expect to be shot at by enemies - even by friends. The problem with success is when you climb that ladder of success you have to step on the fingers of some of your friends who are trying hard just to stay at the same level. People hate those who win more than the average amount of success - whatever their average is. If you think men will swear at you for winning, God save you from the screaming wives!"

Gen. Patton would pause for the laughter to stop, "Every wife wants her husband to be a commander although she will not let give a command in his own home. So when you ride the roller-coaster of life to a high point, always be prepared for the down slope. This is one of the problems of we silly humans. We want people to win, but we get jealous when they do. That is human nature which has not changed in the last ten thousand years. There is little chance that we will change in the next ten thousand years," Gen. Patton concluded.

One day he used the no-change in our human nature idea and applied it to nations. This was after we had a long briefing on Hitler and the way the "blind" German people were following Hitler. Gen. Patton rambled, "Looks like the nature of nations never changes any more than human nature. Give people a nation with lots of freedom, and the people will try to get some dictator to tell them what to do. When people have a dictator, they want freedom. Helps me to understand Thomas Jefferson's remark that the tree of liberty has to be fertilized every few years with the blood of patriots. Trouble is we have so few true patriots. So many give lip service about being a patriot, but when the shooting starts they want to stay home."

It was from Gen. Patton that I learned the true story about Benedict Arnold. Gen. Patton shocked me one day by saying, "Damn fine commander that Benedict Arnold. He was too successful; won too many battles. Congress turned him into a traitor. That Continental Congress was about the same as our present Congress."

Gen. Patton told us of the black shield hanging on the wall of the Chapel at the West Point Military Academy. "That black shield does not have a name on it. All of the other shields for our great generals give their names. That black shield is a memorial to a great commander who did not learn that the first enemy is always our own Congress! Always remember that!"

After the war I researched the life of Benedict Arnold. As usual, I learned that Gen. Patton was correct in all that he had said. Arnold did have a great military record. Arnold won battles in the Revolutionary War which he was not supposed to win! In fact, Gen. Gates removed Arnold from command during the Second Battle of Freeman's Farm.

Gen. Gates was a politically appointed general about

192

the same nature as our National Guard colonel who wanted to go to war with two wives and air conditioning! Rank during the Revolutionary War depended on the number of men you could enlist, or the friends you had in the Continental Congress.

Gen. Gates ordered his troops to retreat. Gen. Arnold was so enraged that he rode his horse into the retreating American troops. The troops followed Arnold's commands and turned the tide of the battle against the British. All of the time Gen. Arnold was defeating the British, an Aide for Gen. Gates was chasing Arnold trying to tell him he would be court-martialled for disobeying Gen. Gates's orders. Gates was far from the front writing to Congress on his reason for retreating. When the battle was won, Gates took all of the credit in a report to the Continental Congress."

When Gen. Patton gave a new idea, he paused frequently for our minds to catch up before continuing, "The cowardly traitor in this battle was Gen. Gates! However, credit for the victory was given to Gates and not to Arnold. Gen. Arnold did not have time to write to Congress! This victory by Gen. Arnold led to the surrender of the British troops at Saratoga. Since Gen. Arnold exposed a favorite of the Continental Congress, promotions for Gen. Arnold were delayed despite Gen. Washington's protests."

Gen. Patton concluded, "Gen. Arnold lost faith that the thirteen colonies could ever become a nation when the Congressmen had interests only in personal gains and not the welfare of the new Country."

An officer asked, "Wasn't Gates the man who wanted Gen. Washington's title of Commander-in-Chief?"

"He was the one! He was constantly asking

Congress to kick Washington out of command."

The officer asked again, "What happened to Gates after Saratoga?"

Gen. Patton answered, "He wrangled out of Congress the title of, Commander-in-Chief for the Southern troops. Not much fighting in the south; 'Gates' type of war. He failed even in this command. Gen. Washington's staff was ready to court-martial him. As I remember he resigned."

Gen. Patton at other times made comments about Gen. Arnold, such as, "Never make the mistake Benedict Arnold made. Never give up serving our Country no matter how many promotions or pay hikes you are cheated out of. Always remember we do not serve Congressmen. We serve Our Great Country. Remember that! We will be a great Country despite all that Congress does to destroy us. Understand that politicians never lose any votes by attacking the military in peacetime. Heaven knows, I should be able to understand this! After World War I, money for the military was cut to almost nothing; such as five hundred dollars for research on a better tank. A good polo pony would cost more than that! I served for years on end without any promotion!"

A colonel asked, "General, exactly what do you mean by 'serving the Country?' Congress is part of the Country. We dare not say anything unfavorable against a Congressmen or we can be court-martialled. Am I right or wrong about this. Lt. Williamson? You should know as our JAG."

Lucky for me I did know and answered, "That is correct. Army Regulations state that we should not speak unkindly about any Congressman. That includes the President and Vice-President."

Success is How You
Bounce When You Hit Bottom

A few months earlier I had been a civilian candidate for public office along with the minority leader of Congress who lived in our Congressional District. I had made many unkind remarks about my friends opponent. When I was called to active military duty, I was amazed to read that Article of War about any unfavorable remarks about Congressman. That Article included no arm waving or gestures of disrespect! Articles of War were the civil and criminal laws for the military. Gen. Patton continued, "Never any unkind words against Congressmen despite what they do to the military and your promotion. But remember this! We serve the Constitution and are commissioned by the President; not by Congress. Remember your oath when you were commissioned? You took an oath to God 'to support the Constitution against all enemies, foreign and domestic.' We serve this Constitution. We do not offer to give our lives for any man - not even the President. Especially not for a Congressman! This is what I mean by serving our Country, colonel."

It is fortunate that Gen. Patton's comments about Congress were not picked up by the reporters, or perhaps too many of his remarks were picked up - which would explain why Gen. Patton missed several promotions in World War II.

At the time I did not fully understand Gen. Patton's linking Congressmen with domestic enemies. I had entered military service from public office. I knew several Congressmen. I could not believe that our first enemy was Congress as Gen. Patton said so often.

One evening I had the chance to ask Gen. Patton about one Congressmen, the man I had campaigned with in Indiana. Gen. Patton explained his thinking, "As individuals, Congressmen are as good as any cross-section of our Country. The problem is they spend too much time getting re-elected and not enough time thinking about the Country."

At that time I was much younger and could not believe men would put their own personal interests ahead of the Country.

My mind went back to Gen. Patton many years later (1984) when I was watching a television program on the news. This TV news commentator was respected by millions of American people. I could not believe his final words about his "personal" interest; television.

His words on the national network were, "Democracies will come and go, but television will be here forever!"

I hope this commentator's words did not intend the meaning which he gave me. I hope he did not mean, "Forget the Country, get a story for TV." However, when our Country was founded, some men were more interested in personal gain than the best interest of the Country. The main interest of the media is more sales of newspapers or gains in television ratings.

One evening I was with Gen. Patton and Col. Devine in Gen. Patton's tent. Col. Devine (later Lieutenant General Devine) had been an instructor at West Point. Gen. Patton enjoyed religious discussions. I was included because I was of a different generation and was more of a "civilian." Even worse, a political office holder! They probed me for "civilian" ideas. Gen. Patton made some comment about "the roller-coaster" of life and launched into religion. "Jesus was always helping the little person who was on the bottom of his luck. Jesus never spent much time talking about those on the top of success except to tell them they should try to do something other than measure their success by how much money they could get. Preachers preach about the Golden Rule as if it was written to help their church. Hell! The Golden Rule is not to make a super-Hitler type of society of do-gooders. Jesus was interested in the little person who had lost all hope. You do unto others, not for the sake of the other person, but because the way you treat others is the way you are going to be treated. The Golden Rule should be written, 'What you do unto others is the way you are going to be done unto!' Or as Ben Franklin said, 'If rascals knew how much money they could make by being righteous, the rascals would become righteous through pure rascality!' That's a part of the Golden Rule! It makes us puzzle over whether we are rascals or righteous, for God's sake!"

It was never possible to tell exactly when Gen. Patton was profane and when he was speaking directly in prayer to God!

Since Gen. Patton related so many minor details of historic battles, I assumed that he secured the facts from his study of history. In talking with Mrs. Ruth Ellen Patton Totten, the Generals's daughter, she told me her father often related facts about battles which he could not have learned from reading history. It was this "recall" of such exact details that confirmed her belief that her father was "reincarnated," or had lived several different lives on this earth. Gen. Patton never mentioned reincarnation to me nor to Col. Devine as we discussed religion. This caused me to believe that he did not believe in reincarnation. After talking with Mrs. Totten, I am puzzled over what Gen. Patton believed.

Many years later, as I researched the life of Benedict Arnold, my mind kept searching for a "big brown animal" which Gen. Patton had mentioned in talking about

Success is How You
Bounce When You Hit Bottom

Gen. Benedict Arnold and the battle at Freeman's Farm.
Gen. Patton had knowledge of the details of every battle
fought any place any time in the history of the world. I
remember Gen. Patton saying that "Arnold won this battle
of Freeman's Farm riding a big brown horse, a big animal,
which he borrowed. His own horse had been shot out from
under him."

I searched and searched the story of this Freeman's
Farm Battle with the hope of finding something about a
"big brown horse." The best I could get was a mention
that Arnold had a horse shot out from under him; no
mention of color or size! I am certain about one thing.
Should I ever meet Benedict Arnold in any hereafter, I am
going to ask, "What was the color of that horse you
borrowed to ride into the Battle of Freeman's Farm!" If he
should answer that he rode "a big brown horse," I will be
convinced that Gen. Patton fought at this battle in one of
his other lives.

After long conversations with Gen. Patton in or near
his tent, I would walk to my tent and meditate over Gen.
Patton's statements. My tent mate was usually gone. With
other officers, he would be in Palm Springs. These
officers teased me about being compelled "to stay after
school" with Gen. Patton. They teased, "If you didn't
have that law degree, you could go with us to Palm
Springs!"

I enjoyed the evening discussions with Gen. Patton
but often regretted that I could not be in Palm Springs with
the other officers.

One evening Gen. Patton touched on the judge-not
rule of the Bible, saying, "Never try to judge others
because to judge others is exactly the way you are going to
be judged. You call a man a crook, he is sure to call you

a crook in return. We get the same as we dish out. I know from some of the names I have called others! However, religion is not for society, nor should it be. It is for the individual. Jesus never talked about any new deal or new society for man. He always talked of how the little guy could improve his position in life."

Gen. Patton brought everything down to the common level with the words, "What do you expect when you hit the top? You think you are better than Jesus? Look what happened to Him? He judged others so he was killed! How can we expect anything any better?"

Gen. Patton cautioned, "Remember, you may think you are defeated when it is only the mind that is defeated!"

Every thing he said was influenced by war. He said, "Being in the Army is like being in life, you cannot quit! The only way out of the Army in time of war is the same as with life, by death! When you hit bottom in life or in a battle, bounce back as high and as fast as you can. People in life are damn funny! People love a successful man. They love heros. And they love to take a hero and cut him to shreds. Seems to make the people feel stronger if they can cut up their hero. And they love a martyr! I know since I have been both a hero and a martyr several times. People love the underdog until that dog gets on top. Then they enjoy tearing the 'top dog' back down to their size or lower. All of this is the reason I insist that success is how high you can bounce when you hit bottom!"

The script writers for the Patton movie caught this idea when they gave George Scott the final words of the movie, PATTON, "All glory is fleeting!"

ALWAYS KEEP SOMETHING IN RESERVE

This principle might seem to conflict with Gen. Patton's constant driving everything to exhaustion, but Gen. Patton always kept something in reserve. His best reserve was his driving will to win.

We never prepared any battle plan without at least one alternate plan. We had to do all of the work for all of the plans so that a change could be made quickly. In addition we had to have add-on plans that were to be followed when one plan was finished. Any plan for regrouping or consolidating was done on the move.

In the Patton movie, the scenes of the Battle of the Bulge were not fiction. The situation with the Allied Forces was extremely grave. The German attack could have destroyed our entire invasion force if the drive had gone through to the landing sites. This was the intention of Hitler's hard core troops in their final effort. The weather was bitter cold with wind and blinding snow.

In the movie, as on the battle field, Gen. Eisenhower called a meeting of his top commanders. He briefed his army commanders, "We have several hundred men holding out against the enemy. If these troops surrender, the enemy could get completely behind our lines and cause havoc with our supply lines. The weather is too bad for us to get any supply by air. We must get ammunition and food to these besieged troops. How soon can any of you move your troops to give support in this critical situation?"

Gen. Eisenhower was expecting a reply measured in a number of days. Gen. Patton answered, "Our Third Army will start moving the minute I put through a call to my Chief of Staff, Gen. Gay."

Gen. Eisenhower and the other commanders

chuckled at Gen. Patton, thinking it was another one of Gen. Patton's brash statements. The other Army Commanders were fighting the weather. Gen. Patton and his troops were always trying to get a chance to fight the enemy.

Gen. Patton answered their chuckling with profanity, saying, "Give me that field telephone. We've been expecting this attack from the Germans. Look at our intelligence reports we have sent to your staff, Ike. We told you the attack would be coming. Give me that damn telephone!"

Gen. Patton called his headquarters and the Third Army moved immediately. The Battle of the Bulge commander for the Allied force answered the demand for surrender with the word, "Nuts" which the Germans interpreted to mean, "Go to hell!"

Even before the weather cleared, the Third Army raced to attack. Hitler's last drive was turned into defeat.

After the war I talked with Gen. Gay about this scene in the Patton movie. He commented, "It was terrible winter weather. When Gen. Patton left for Ike's headquarters, he ordered us to be ready to move immediately. You remember how tight the alert was when we were waiting to dash into Mexico to meet the Japs? Well, it was the same in Germany except there was no sleeping on the ground as we did in the desert. We knew the Germans were planning this attack, and we told Ike's staff it would be coming. As usual, Gen. Patton's estimate of the situation was correct. It was so cold it was no task at all to keep the men awake and hugging together around the fires. Our camps looked like a shanty town with the tarp shelters draped over the men and trucks. The wind was blowing so hard a man could not be exposed to the wind for many minutes.

Always Keep Something In Reserve

Unlike Gen. Patton, Gen. Gay talked slowly. He continued, "We ordered that every engine be started every fifteen minutes to make sure we could roll as soon as we received the orders from Ike. Some of the engines were never stopped. I knew Gen. Patton would be calling since we knew all of the other armies would be unable to move. We had three plans we could have used depending on where Ike's headquarters wanted us to attack. As soon as Gen. Patton called and said, 'Plan 1', I held up one finger to the commanders in my trailer. Before I finished talking to the General, the engines of the tanks and trucks were roaring so loud I could barely hear the General. When the weather is so cold, men prefer to be doing something rather than sitting around a fire. We rolled towards the enemy so fast that in the blowing snow, I am sure the enemy thought we were German tanks!"

Many historians have written about Gen. Patton's ability to speed men into combat. It is my opinion a greater talent was his ability to change battle plans quickly. I remember some of Gen. Patton's words at some of the briefing sessions, "We must be able to move around like a boxer. The faster we move the easier it will be to kill the enemy. When we cannot change our battle plans to fit the situation, it is the same as digging a foxhole. We will never let the enemy catch us sitting! We have to be able to change or we will get the hell shot out of us. We would deserve it! When we are not moving, we are losing. Nothing ever stays the same in war."

Any commander or staff officer who could not or would not make rapid changes would be transferred. I remember one colonel who insisted, "General Patton, we have been doing this maneuver this way for years!"

"That's the trouble with your plan! We must always be making changes so the enemy will have no idea what we are going to do! We must be able to change our plans every hour and on any hour of the day or night!"

Although Gen. Patton would drive to the last drop of gasoline, he always had an alternate plan in reserve.

REVENGE BELONGS TO GOD

There was never an hour in our lives with Gen. Patton that we were not building hatred for the enemy, but we never trained for revenge. Gen. Patton respected the enemy and admired some of their generals. He never discussed destroying the enemy for the sake of revenge.

The enemy soldiers were to be hated and killed as the only way to save our lives. We were lectured on the importance of killing the enemy to bring about the end of the war. War was a game of life and death. Men had to be trained to kill to win the war.

It is true that Gen. Patton said, "I cannot see any good reason for taking any prisoners - alive!" Such words were used to build up hatred for the enemy. Prisoners taken by Gen. Patton's troops were treated better than most prisoners because Gen. Patton's men had better than average treatment at all times.

I remember one staff conference when Gen. Patton stopped a colonel in the middle of a sentence. The colonel was reporting, "We are low on gasoline and supplies. They have plenty available if Washington would only get off their duff and get some shipments to us. We can slow down our training and get even with Washington. If they cause us delays, we can show them how to really delay a program. We can get revenge ..."

Gen. Patton cut the colonel's conversation, "Colonel, revenge belongs to God. We do not try to get revenge against anybody to get our supplies. Get on the phone and make Washington move! If we cannot get our supplies, we will go with what we've got. If we go out of our way for revenge, we may never get our supplies. Revenge belongs to God!"

Gen. Patton was silent as the colonel sulked. Gen.

smiled and said, "I am not at all sure that God could be of any help in Washington, but He could do more to straighten them out than we could."

Those words, "Revenge belongs to God," were etched in my mind. It would be several years before I discovered the words were from the Bible. These words fit the general pattern of Gen. Patton's principles. It matched, "Don't fight a battle if you do not gain anything when you win." Nothing would be gained by merely getting revenge against Washington. It could be in getting revenge we would handicap our programs.

Years later I remembered this revenge principle when I was under attack in civilian life by a political enemy who was using every trick in the book to destroy me and my professional reputation. There were many things I could have done in revenge, but Gen. Patton's words held me back.

Early one morning my alarm-radio awakened me with a news program. The first story on the news was about my political enemy. My political enemy had hung himself! Revenge belonged to God! God had taken care of my enemy in a most severe fashion. Gen. Patton's words came back to me, "Leave a few things to God. Go for revenge, you may destroy yourself."

DEATH CAN BE MORE EXCITING THAN LIFE

Gen. Patton destroyed the fear of death with his deep religious faith and his keen sense of humor. He pictured death as the greatest thrill of life! I am convinced that he was sincere when he said that he prayed that God would take his life in combat. I remember his saying so often, "I would like to die by the last bullet fired at the last battle of the last war!"

In the Patton movie several minutes were given to portraying Gen. Patton as having a belief in reincarnation. Never in any discussion did I ever hear him say that he believed in reincarnation. Often he said that there were no new battles to be fought. Every form and type of battle had been fought in the thousands of years of our existence. There could not be any changes in the type of battle, only the type of weapons would change. I am sure Gen. Patton had studied every battle reported in any of our history books including the Bible. He spent his life visiting battlefields. For him to say, as George Scott did in the movie, "I've been on this battle field before," did not mean that he believed in reincarnation. It meant that he had studied the battle area in great detail and had walked the ground where the battle had been fought.

Gen. Patton's daughter, Ruth Ellen Patton Totten, is convinced that her father could recall exact details of events which happened in his other lives. She reasoned that he would remember facts which he had not read but that would be confirmed by later research by others. She related events of her father serving as a soldier under Napoleon in the winter attack on Russia. Also, his life as a soldier in the Battle at Gettysburg. Gen. Patton recalled experiences when serving in the Roman Legions. According to the daughter, "Only God knows how many lives Gen. Patton has lived."

As I stated earlier, I am puzzled over the "the big animal, the big brown horse" which Gen. Arnold rode in the Battle of Freeman's Farm. When Gen. Patton told the story of this battle he spoke as if from personal knowledge. I continue to be puzzled over whether Gen. Patton could be reincarnated. As I mention at the close of this book, I heard a radio program coming from Seattle, Washington, while driving in Oklahoma. By an unusual quirk in the sky and the radio waves, I could hear this radio program over a thousand miles from the station. Such a radio wave seldom is able to reach over a hundred miles. The radio program was an interview with a descendant of the Indian Chief, Seattle. The mystery of this program is that by letter and telephone, I have been unable to locate any descendant of Chief Seattle nor any radio station that has any knowledge of such a program. Could it be that Gen. Patton is reincarnated as Chief Seattle?

The daughter confirmed that her father had two heroes; Christ and Alexander. I remember her saying with laughter, "No doubt he would put Alexander ahead of Christ since Alexander was a better soldier!"

I am sure the daughter is correct because Gen. Patton talked of how it was poor strategy for Christ to walk into the camp of his enemies. Col. Devine explained that Jesus was following the scriptures. Gen. Patton argued, "If so, why did he weaken on the cross and ask, 'Father, why have you forsaken me!' He weakened when he should have been strong!"

In reading the life of Alexander I learned that he wore a shiny helmet! Alexander was seen by his troops every day; always near the front. He offered to settle the war with Persia in a personal duel with Darius, King of Persia. Alexander was concerned with the welfare of his troops.

Gen. Patton wore a shiny helmet and was constantly seeking the best food for his troops. Gen. Patton wore his pistols and told every soldier he was going to kill Hitler. Gen. Patton talked with the soldiers and was always near the front. He did see any need for so many fine American young men to die in war. He believed the way to settle a war would be for the leaders to battle; the victor would be declared the winner of the war.

To add to the mystery, Alexander claimed a close relationship with Zeus, the supreme God of ancient Greece. Could it be that Gen. Patton talked of reincarnation to generate a belief in the troops that he, Gen. Patton, had a close relationship with some supreme power? No one could doubt that Gen. Patton often spoke to God - asking and insisting on good fighting weather! I am sure that if Gen. Patton gave a moment of thought to the idea that to be reincarnated would give the soldiers more faith in him and in their chance of winning, he would believe in reincarnation!

Gen. Patton seldom mentioned that he was an Episcopalian. One time I repeated President Lincoln's religious idea; namely, "I will join any church that has as its only creed, the Golden Rule. That, and only that church will I join and none other." Gen. Patton commented, "That's my kind of religion!"

No one ever doubted that Gen. Patton believed in God. His religion was good for all seven days of the week. He did not limit his religion for show on Sunday although he attended Sunday chapel services with the troops.

The first Sunday we were in the Desert Training Center, Gen. Patton ordered a church service. We did not have a chapel, chairs, altar, or anything, but we had a chapel service. The area in front of Gen. Patton's tent became the altar with the American Flag in the center of the service. Standing erect in the front row of troops for this first service was Gen. Patton.

I never heard Gen. Patton pray. I remember him saying quite often, "Your life is a prayer! God is everywhere in all of us. This idea that Christ is going to return in nonsense! God is present in all of us every day. Remember that a true friend is a glimpse of God. No need to look up to some God in the sky or look at your shoes for your sins. God is in all of us!"

Gen. Patton respected our Army Chaplains and had them attend all important staff meetings. He was always calling on the Chaplains to "get a hot line to God!" During the Battle of the Bulge, when the winter weather was so terrible, he ordered the Chaplain to get a prayer to God that would change the weather! This prayer is repeated,

> "Restrain these immoderate storms, grant us fair weather for battle, graciously harken to us as soldiers who call upon The, that armed with Thy power, we may advance from victory to victory and establish Thy justice among men and nations!"

This prayer was "sent up" on December 12, 1944. It took God a few days to clear the weather, and the soldiers did "advance from victory to victory."

Gen. Patton's religious faith came through to us in his many references to death. He knew that death was the constant fear of every soldier. Thus, he was constantly trying to destroy this fear by saying, "Did you ever stop to think how much more exciting death will be than life? We know what it is like to live on this earth. We do not know

209

what it will be like to live after death. Take a good look at Nature. No way you can fail to believe in life after death when you study Nature!" His lectures gave us more confidence and religion than any church sermon.

We were all impressed with Gen. Patton's knowledge of the Bible. One of his biographers wrote that Gen. Patton could identify by chapter and verse more quotations than any international Bible scholar. For Gen. Patton the Bible was a series of stories of combat.

I remember his explanation of fear and faith. We were nearing the longest day of the year, June 21, 1942. Col. Gay and I were walking towards Gen. Patton's tent. There was a red glow on the western clouds. Gen. Patton was outside of his tent and said, "Damn fine sunset. Makes you feel great to see such a sight. Everything hanging in balance in the universe for a sunset like that. Just like fear and faith. You get too many fears, you have to find the faith to match the fears. You get too much faith, and you will get more fears to test your faith. God keeps trying to build us up to conquer all fears including death. He never gives us more fears than we can conquer, though. If we give up and fall down with our fears, somehow He will pick us up and give us enough faith to match our next fears. If we never give up we can destroy all of our fears. God runs both the fear and the faith departments. If there ever was a devil, God could destroy him easily. God does not fail at anything. Fear and faith grow together. If you do not have the faith to face death, not much chance you will have enough faith to live a full life. Many of us live half alive and half dead. No beauty in that! Nothing like that great sunset!"

"You see all of that in the sunset, General?" Col. Gay asked.

"All that and more! Well, not really. I just see a

small part of the universe, but any power that put this universe together had a great battle plan." We watched silently as the sun kept changing the colors on the Chuckawalla Mountain Range.

Every soldier knew that Gen. Patton was concerned about him. If the soldier was afraid of combat and death, there was no need to worry because Gen. Patton admitted being scared. The way to whip fear was to keep going forward! Gen. Patton said so. The troops were as loyal to Gen. Patton as he was to them. This devotion of the troops was difficult for strangers to understand. Strangers could not believe that men could be so loyal to a commander who was so hard and demanded so much. Gen. Patton demanded death for every soldier if it was necessary for victory, but Gen. Patton would be the first to give his life.

The stories and legends about Gen. Patton were unlimited even in 1942. I remember one newspaper reporter who told me was going to write a full story on the Patton myth of the troops loving their commander. This reporter was on the staff of a large national newspaper chain. How he managed to dodge the draft was a subject he would not discuss. I was assigned to accompany this reporter for his tour of the Desert Training Center. He asked our jeep driver to stop when he saw a rifleman jumping up and down on the starter of his motorcycle. This soldier would make a good candidate for the reporter to question about the myth of the soldiers' loyalty to Gen. Patton.

After a few preliminary questions about the soldier's name and home town, the reporter asked, "Do you think Gen. Patton will go to heaven when he dies?"

The soldier answered immediately without stopping his efforts to start his motorcycle, "He will go to heaven if he wants to, but not until he is ready!"

The reporter wanted more from the soldier; hence, he continued to question, "Do you think it possible Gen. Patton will go to hell?"

The soldier was getting angry with both the reporter and the motorcycle. He said in disgust, "Look! With Gen. Patton anything and everything is possible. If he decided he wanted to go to hell, I sure would like to go with him!" The reporter shook his head in disbelief. We returned to base camp.

Many stories were told about Gen. Patton and the loyalty of his troops. The men enjoyed his lectures, his humor, his laughing at himself and making them laugh with him. I always liked the story about a member of Gen. Marshall's staff who asked a second lieutenant if he believed that Gen. Patton could walk on water.

The lieutenant replied, "Colonel, I know Gen. Patton. If you gave him an order to walk on water, he would figure out a way, and within twenty-four hours he would have me doing it!" This story made the rounds of the dining halls for months.

The story Gen. Patton liked the best of all those told about him is the answer of the soldier who was asked if the soldier believed that Gen. Patton was so great that he would arise from his grave after three days.

The answer, "Hell no! Gen. Patton would not arise from the grave after three days! Anything he was going to do he would do in less than three days!"

I remember Gen. Patton discussing heaven. He reasoned, "We know so little about heaven. It is supposed to be the best of everything. If so, why should be we be scared to die? God can whip the devil any day of the week. I am amused at those preachers who stand in the pulpit and preach about the glory of heaven but are scared to die. Give these preachers a touch of slight pain, and they may die from fright. If heaven is so great, why would such types be so scared? Looks like they would welcome a chance to get into heaven a few years early! Why hesitate? One thing I know, death is going to be something. " He gave his boyish smile and added, "At least death will be different than life. I am sure that death will be exciting because it is only a phase in the cycle of life.!"

BETTER TO FIGHT FOR SOMETHING IN LIFE
THAN DIE FOR NOTHING

Gen. Patton was always laughing at death, and the troops laughed with him. Many of his talks to the troops provoked laughter, but his messages were remembered.

"We are lucky people!" He lectured, "We are in war! We have a chance to fight and die for something. A lot of people never get that chance! Think of all of the poor people you know that have lived and died for nothing. Total lives spent doing nothing but eating, sleeping, and going to work until the retirement watch is received. Nothing to die for! We are lucky that we are fighting a war that will change the history of the world. If we live, we can put our grandchildren on our knees and tell them how we won the war. If we die, our friends will tell how we died to make life better for them. If you are going to die, might as well die a hero! If you kill enough people before you die, they might name a street after you!" The troops laughed.

Whether the thinking was reasonable or not, the men remembered Gen. Patton's words.

He never gave the usual commander's pre-combat talk such as, "If we keep alert, we will all come out of this alive. Do not take any chances. We have lived through combat before and we will make it through again."

Such untruth was not for Gen. Patton. He always spoke the harsh brutal truth. "Some of us are going to die, but we are tough enough to take a dozen of the enemy before we go. The enemy cannot kill all of us. As long as any one of us remains alive, we'll keep killing the bastards. Our chances of living in war are much better than trying to live on our highways at home. We can get killed on the highway and die for nothing. I would rather be shot dead through the head with an enemy bullet than to have my head bashed into a automobile windshield. When we die in war, we will always be remembered. We will never be heros for being killed on our highways at home. When we can take life and death and not get scared by either, we can whip anything."

Today, I am sure many would say that Gen. Patton brain-washed his men. If so, there are many Americans that need a good brain-washing. Helping people face life and death follows the basic laws of Nature. There is no brain-wash in the truth of Gen. Patton's words, "Every day of life is one day closer to death." Gen. Patton constantly stressed the cold hard truth of war; namely, if we do not kill the enemy, the enemy will kill us. This is a truth which those that pray for peace do not understand. Everyone wants peace. The confusion is over whether there will ever be peace when there is preaching and picketing by those in fear of death.

The troops laughed when Gen. Patton said, "When you see you are going to be killed, you might as well kill a dozen of the bastards before they get you. Why not? You would save us the trouble!" His timing on such remarks was perfect. "You may not get killed; only shot! You may collect a bit of lead which could cause a hole that might improve the circulation of your system! For that Washington will give you an award, the Purple Heart! Get hit three times and you could get three medals to wear. Get enough medals and it will make you stronger just to wear them around!"

When he made these speeches his chest was filled with the many awards which he had received including the Purple Heart. He said so many times, "A soldier in this army will die only once! Cowards and draft dodgers die many times every day!"

This last thought did not originate with Gen. Patton, but he supported the reasoning with cold hard truth. He always attempted to face truth; grab it by the nose. I remembered Gen. Patton's words when I was with eleven combat trained fighter pilots on a train to Florida from the advanced flight center at Williams Field, Arizona. We had been screened carefully to be a new breed of pilots; night fighter pilots. We would be flying at night and in bad weather. I was the senior officer of the group. We had been screened with super medical and physical examinations plus tests for night vision. All that we were told was that we would be using airborne radar.

Radar was so secret we were unable to gain even the slightest bit of information about what we would be doing. We had heard that the British had been using radar to attack the German bomber formations. We guessed that "radar" had something to do with radio, but we were not sure. It would be several weeks before we were briefed that radar was the code word for "radio detection and ranging." We were told we would be hunting for enemy planes always at night and in bad weather using radar.

Every one of us had volunteered for this new night fighter program. We knew that some of the tests we had to take had nothing to do with physical ability or vision. Sitting alone in a black box for over an hour was a test for something we knew would be different

One afternoon on the train, one of the young pilots came to me with a problem with his local draft board. He had a letter advising him that his local draft board was drafting him for military service. The problem was his local draft board had given him the draft board classification of 4F which meant that he was physically

Better To Fight For Something In Life
Than Die For Nothing

unfit for military service. His local draft board knew he had been in an auto accident which resulted brain surgery; a metal plate had been placed in his head. He wanted to be in the military service so he drove to another state and enlisted without saying a word about the metal plate! Draft boards had quotas to fill! When this pilot's home-town draft board learned he was in the service, they put his name on their draft list to help them fill their quota. They needed every name they could get. They wanted him to return and be drafted from his home town!

I remember his question to me, "Is there anything wrong with my being from both states? I don't care which state gets credit for my enlisting."

As we discussed this problem with the other pilots, I learned that no one was physically qualified for military service! Yet, all of us had passed the physical exam for flight training and night fighter combat pilot duty! I did not have a metal plate in my head, but I had suffered a skull fracture which put me "out" for more days than the number of days the military would accept.

One of the pilots recalled the last line of our physical examination form, "Remember that last line of the physical which the docs made us sign? My doctor put down, 'Denies all else.' Wonder how much they knew?" We laughed that we had fooled the doctors by refusing to admit that we had any other illnesses or disabilities. Perhaps the doctors were not fooled. The doctors knew we were going on some unknown missions. They knew they had to select some "fools" that wanted to fight for something.

Unlike Gen. Patton, I did have any desire to die in combat. However, I would not turn away from any assignment because it was too dangerous. I did not want somebody taking a mission which I might have the physical ability to take. This was not a desire te be super-brave. Probably the desire was to give no one the chance to say I turned away from any "calculated risk" of war.

"More people die in bed than in war!" Gen. Patton explained. "Going to bed is like digging a foxhole. It is easy for death to catch you asleep! The Lord said, 'Pick up your bed and walk!' Staying in bed is the same as staying in a swivel chair too long. The brain gets clogged and the body gets sick. Next thing you know some doctor will load you up with pills that are supposed to get everything back in order. Just moving around could do more for you than a whole handful of pills!"

The troops laughed. On the staff we thought Gen. Patton was pushing too far. Many years later doctors would start having their surgical patients "picking up their beds and walking" a day or two after surgery.

I did not see the full importance of Gen. Patton's idea until I visited nursing homes after the war. Many of the nursing homes reminded me of Gen. Patton's words, "Dash out and meet death on your own terms!" It would be years before society would start thinking that perhaps people should have the right to die on their own terms and not be nursed to death for twenty years as a vegetable. The heavy doses of sleeping pills keep the senior citizens as immobile as potted plants.

I remember Gen. Patton saying, "A lot of people die at forty but are not buried until thirty years later. Many people have a short tour with an illness and give up and die at an early age. They go from doctor to doctor until death catches them in bed."

In 1942 Gen. Patton was preaching that if you did not keep moving around the juices would never get to the right places. Gen. Patton's death was proof of this truth. He did not die from a broken neck resulting from an auto accident. He died from the accumulation of liquids in his lungs and heart. The juices were not going to the right places. God has my sympathy for being compelled to suffer Gen. Patton's wrath for death in an auto accident.

Medical science has advanced rapidly, but there is no pill as strong as Gen. Patton's advice, "Settle with death on your own terms!" So few people face the truth that we all have a terminal illness; age. So many people die young and are buried years later. Many of us want to argue with death which only hastens death. Many of us are so afraid of death that we lack the courage to have the physical examination which could catch some terminal illness - other than old age for which there is no cure.

FEAR KILLS MORE PEOPLE THAN DEATH!

When I heard Gen. Patton say, "Fear kills more people than death," I smiled because I did not catch the full impact of his words. When I heard these words later I noticed the troops were silent. I puzzled over how many men understood what Gen. Patton was saying. No minister I have ever heard put life-after-death in such simple and blunt terms.

Today when I quote this principle, many people think the principle is as foolish as I did when I first heard it. One soldier retorted, "Death is death, isn't it?"

But death was not death for Gen. Patton. With the faith to destroy all fears, death will be a phase in the cycle of life as Gen. Patton said so often. Gen. Patton's principle is in the words, "Those in fear will die a thousand deaths." I remember Gen. Patton saying, "A coward is always in hell because he will suffer a thousand deaths every day. A brave soldier dies only once; death is only a phase in the cycle of life."

The soldiers told and retold many stories about what would happen when Gen. Patton died. Every soldier knew that Gen. Patton wanted to give his life in combat. We loved him for doing what he asked of us and because he was so concerned about every one of us. No one expected him to live forever. The stories about his death started years before the fatal auto accident. So many times he related how much better it would be to die in combat than in some stupid auto accident.

The soldiers told a story of his death before he was killed in a minor auto accident. Arriving at the Gates of Heaven, Gen. Patton demanded to know where he could locate God. In the presence of God, Gen. Patton exploded, "What in the name of hell is the idea of having me die in an auto accident? How unkind of you to pick me off in an auto accident. I prayed to you to take my life in combat. An auto accident is no way for a soldier to die! Give me orders to go to hell. I do not belong here! I do not want to face my own brave soldiers who have earned their place in Heaven."

According to the soldiers' story, God answered, "If you want to go to hell it can be arranged! Gen. Patton saluted, clicked his heels, did a sharp about face and walked away.

God called to him, "Gen. Patton, giving your request serious thought, I want you to reconsider and stay with us."

Gen. Patton protested, I do not belong here. I am going to hell where I belong!"

God protested, "I do not want you to go to hell. I want you to stay. If you go to hell, it will be only a few weeks until you destroy the devil, put out all of the fires of hell, and my people will leave heaven to be with you. Please, stay for Heaven's sake!"

Gen. Patton hesitated so God added, "And we will let you wear your uniform and pistols any time you wish!"

There was another story of Gen. Patton death's and his visit to Heaven. The story was about Gen. Patton pressing the doorbell of the Gates of Heaven. No one answered. Gen. Patton pounded on the door with his fist. St. Peter finally arrived dressed in toga and sandals.

Gen. Patton exploded, "Why were you not here at the gate? Don't you know your assigned duty? Didn't you ever read the Bible? You belong at this gate twenty-four hours of the day! What kind of uniform is that? Look at your feet? You could never run a mile in such sandals. What happened to your razor? When did you have your last shave? Where is your necktie? Where is your helmet?"

There were so many stories. The laughter of the troops displayed the total devotion of the troops to their commander.

Gen. Patton's thoughts about death were not unlike those of Churchill who said in 1941, "It is a good time to live and a good time to die." This matched Gen. Patton's thought that both living and dying could be exciting.

I remember an evening when he compared death to gambling. "Our problem is we do not understand life after death. The whole joy of life is in taking chances to build up enough faith to destroy all fears - including death. That is why gambling is so much fun. The highest gamble of life is in combat with an enemy who wants to kill you. You bet your life on that gamble. You can never gamble with any higher stakes. If we did not have wars for men to gamble on we would find something else." I remember Col. Gay asking, "Where does gambling on fast women fit into that system, General?"

"Many men die from chasing fast women, Hap!" Col. Gay's first name was Hobart. His nick name among his rank and higher was "Hap." I always called him "Colonel!"

Gen. Patton continued, "What do men do when they have a lot of money? They gamble on women, fast cars, hunting wild animals, or something where there is a chance of death! Look at our millionaires who race speed boats. Why do young kids take chances on driving fast cars? They want the thrill of facing death; the greatest thrill of life. Without a lot of money, we all like to watch others defy death on a high trapeze bar or in facing a wild bull in bull fighting. Why? It gives us courage when we see that others are not afraid of death."

One morning in the late summer of 1942, Gen.

Fear Kills More People Than Death!

Patton received a telephone call from Gen. Marshall's office in Washington. Gen. Patton had returned to Washington several times without any special announcement to us. This time it was a solemn Gen. Patton who told us, "Gen. Marshall told me to bring two shirts with me!" Gen. Patton did not smile. "It looks like I will be leaving our I Armored Corps and the desert. It may be I will have a higher staff assignment in Europe but no command."

Many of us, old and young, cried, but this time Gen. Patton did not cry although he often shed tears. Less than a week later, Gen. Patton returned and cried big tears as he told us, "We will never be going into combat as a unit. Our assignment for the war will be to stay here and train others. Many of you will be transferred into new units that will be going overseas. They told me that it would be November before there would be a convoy of ships big enough to get us to North Africa. By November, Rommel will have captured the Suez Canal. It will be a long war. I suppose they think I am too old at fifty-six to be the senior officer of a combat command." He left the briefing room in tears. No one had a dry eye.

The next day he asked four of us, all the lieutenants on his staff, to come to his office. At this time he told us that the Army wanted us to apply for flight training if we could pass the flight physical examination.

I remember his crying as he dismissed us. He cautioned, "Remember what we look like when you fly over us. Drop you bombs on the enemy; not on us. What the hell am I saying? I'll still be here in the desert training troops!"

We protested leaving, but Gen. Patton advised, "This is no place to be when the fighting is on the other side of the ocean! Not for young officers!"

Fear Kills More People Than Death!

Some historians report that Gen. Marshall wanted Gen. Patton to be second in command of the task force which landed in North Africa in November. Gen. Patton refused the command because the troops which would be involved were not ready for combat. Also, Gen. Patton wanted our I Armored Corps to join in the invasion since we were trained for the desert.

After Gen. Patton left the briefing room in Washington, it is reported that Gen. Marshall spoke to his Pentagon staff, "We need Gen. Patton's motivation for this task force, but don't worry. Patton wants a combat command. He knows this could be his last chance to get a combat command."

According to the historians, Gen. Patton called Gen. Marshall and agreed to take the second in command for the North African invasion with poorly trained troops. Our staff never knew of this call to Washington by Gen. Patton. It is unimportant what actually happened. In a few days, Gen. Patton was ordered back to Washington.

The last evening I was with Gen. Patton and Col. Gay we discussed the Carolina maneuvers and the capture of Gen. Drum. Col. Gay had never heard the story of the movement of the fuel by rail and the anger of Gen. Drum.

On the way back to our tents, Col. Gay commented on the capture of Gen. Drum, "Drum kicked Gen. Patton off a polo team in Hawaii for swearing too much, as I have been told. Drum was the commanding general of the military post. Drum did this in front of the whole crowd of people watching the game. Drum told Gen. Patton to ride off the field. Patton saluted and obeyed. As Patton rode off the field so did all of the polo players including the opposing team. Drum had to call all of the polo players from the stables. All of the players vowed they did not hear Gen. Patton swear. Patton was a Captain at the time, I believe. The game was started again with Gen. Patton playing. This increased Gen. Drum's anger over Gen. Patton's getting such support from the public.

Drum was of the old school that wanted to keep everything the same. Drum did not want to see that an armored tank was a better weapon than a horse.

Several months later, as I related earlier, I was preparing to transfer my duties as Squadron Commander of a Night Fighter Pilot training squadron. Our mission in the training squadron was to train pilots and radar observers in the best use of the Black Widow; the plane designed for searching out and attacking enemy planes at night. Our training was primarily in the "courage" to fly at night and in bad weather. The first planes we had were converted A-20s called, p-70s. The next plane was the Black Widow which looked big and dangerous with four rapid-firing twenty millimeter cannons plus machine guns. The problem was it was a single-seater aircraft with no chance for a pilot to get any copilot time before flying solo. The pilot had to learn the "tricks" of the plane on the first solo flight!

As the commanding officer of a new Black Widow squadron to go overseas into combat, I could select my staff, including the pilots, We were sure we could go over and win the war with our new Black Widows!

I was busy selecting the pilots, radar observers, and staff officers when my newly selected Squadron Flight Surgeon came to see me. He ordered, "You are not going overseas until I see an x-ray of your left knee."

This officer had caught me limping and asked to examine my knee. He did not like the lump in my leg. Neither did I! My knee hurt most of the time. The x-ray of my knee revealed a large tumor. It was bone cancer! I was facing death from cancer and not from a plane crash or combat with the enemy; not even from Gen. Patton.

My military career ended with a leg amputation. Bone cancer was considered terminal - no chance of recovery. After months in amputation centers, I returned to the civilian life.

After the war ended in Europe, I wrote to Gen. Patton asking him to visit Indiana when he returned to the States. I wanted to arrange a Victory Parade in Indianapolis for him so that he could get the tributes which he deserved.

My letter to Gen. Patton was dated September 13, 1945. Since my letter would go through several military offices before reaching Gen. Patton, I was amazed to receive a reply in eleven days from the time the letter was mailed. Gen. Patton's letter was dated September 24, 1945. In the letter he stated:

> Many thanks for your good letter of 13 September. I am, unfortunately, completely unable to make any commitments for the future at this time as I have no idea when I shall again be in the United States. With all good wishes on your return to civilian life, I am,
>
> Very truly yours,
> (signed)   G.S. Patton, Jr., General

Six days after Gen. Patton wrote to me, he was relieved of command of his Third Army; the Army which had won the war in Europe. I am sure he knew on September 24th that he was going to be removed from command of the Third Army. Several years later I learned from Gen. Gay how discouraged Gen. Patton was during this period. Gen. Gay was Gen. Patton's Chief of Staff in all of the campaigns in

227

Fear Kills More People Than Death!

Europe. Gen. Gay confirmed that Gen. Patton typed some of his own letters by the hunt-and-peck method. My letter did not have any initials of any clerk-typist. This letter would be my last contact with Gen. Patton.

About sixty days after Gen. Patton wrote to me, he was riding with Gen. Gay when they were in a minor auto accident. Gen. Patton's neck was broken in falling forward into the front seat of the automobile.

There are many stories that Gen. Patton was murdered by some of his enemies. These stories are not true. After the accident Gen. Patton was taken to a field hospital which was an old cavalry barracks. His hospital room "was no wider each way than outstretched arms" according to one of the nurses that attended him. Gen. Patton had around-the-clock nurses and a surgical team in constant attendance. His death was caused by "fluids building up in his lungs and heart," according to the final report. Since he could not move, "the juices could not go to the right places" - the words he gave to us so many times.

Several years later, Gen. Gay was stationed in Chicago as the Commanding General of our Fifth Army. Without an appointment or a telephone call, I stopped at the Fifth Army Headquarters and asked to see the Commanding General. Three stars of a lieutenant general can change some men, but could not change a man of the great caliber of Gen. Gay. Within minutes I was in the General's office, and we were discussing our favorite subject, Gen. Patton.

Gen. Gay commented, "It seems like many years since we were on the General's staff in the desert looking at each other every day across our desks. Seems like more than a century!"

I asked Gen. Gay about how Gen. Patton had died.

Fear Kills More People Than Death!

He answered, "Just a simple auto accident; the type he said was worse than a death in war. All that stuff about the General being assassinated or murdered is pure latrine rumor. God knows he has had more serious accidents in being thrown from horses. I was with him at the time and was with him all the way to the hospital. There was no possible chance he could live. I remember his saying immediately after the accident, 'Hap, I am paralyzed! I cannot feel my hands or feet. I am sure this is it for me!'"

We discussed the death of Gen. Patton's Aide, Lt. Jensen, our friend who was killed in North Africa. Gen. Gay talked of the many problems with the invasion of Germany. He always talked slowly and reviewed every word before he spoke.

Gen. Gay said, "The General told me he had received a letter from you. It was the first we knew you were out of the service with a leg amputation. Except for his family, the letter he wrote to you could have been his last personal letter."

I said I was so sorry to hear of the General's death. I repeated the old story the troops told of Gen. Patton reprimanding God for having him die in an auto accident.

Gen. Gay did not speak for several seconds, "You know . . ." He was silent again. "I am glad the General died when he did. God knew best."

My mouth opened in shock.

Gen. Gay continued, "Do not get the wrong idea. I was as sorry as any. We all lost a great man, and I lost my best friend. Let me explain why God knew best. You know the auto accident was when we were on our way to a game reserve. That hunting trip was my idea. I needed to talk to him away from the office. I wanted the General to retire from the service and return to the States. This was when he mentioned your name. Said you wanted him to return for some tribute from the State of Indiana. He did not oppose me on retiring from the service, but he said he intended to resign and not retire. During his last days his mind had been wandering over the many battles. You remember how he could cry with tears running down his face. Well, he cried when he recounted the thousands of lives that had been lost because of the delays in pursuing the enemy. Yes, we were short of rations, gas, even maps. You see, the General was preparing to write a book about the war. He wanted to document the campaigns and the unnecessary losses caused by the Allied Command playing the war like a political chess game. I agreed with all that he said. His conclusions were correct, but I did not want him to have to go through all of it again in writing a book. I reasoned that he could lose the favor of the American people who loved him. He argued with me and talked of the many political leaders who made the trip to Europe to ask him to run for President - both parties wanted him! Do you remember what he said about politicians when we were in the Desert Training Center?"

I answered, "I remember his saying several times that I was foolish for running for political office, and that he would never be so foolish."

"Yes, he said that, but if he had lived he might have changed his mind. He was so intent on giving the truth to the American people. Honestly, I think he could have been elected President. God knows he had enough money to run a national campaign. I told him he was too honest for politics. You know he could never keep from speaking the truth. Never could! And never did! I am sure he would have had a miserable time in politics, and I told him so."

I mumbled something in agreement. Gen. Gay did not speak for several minutes before finishing, "The General listened to me, but he did not agree. My only success was in getting him to agree to take this fatal hunting trip."

Gen. Gay turned around in his swivel chair with his back to me. Gen. Patton would have been angry if he had caught me with tears in my eyes. I could see Gen. Gay was drying his eyes before he spoke again, "Well, Williamson, God has my sympathy. I am sure the General raised hell in heaven if things were not moving properly up there!"

In the silence which followed I knew there was something which I should say, but I could not find words. I finally said, "He missed the down slope, and I am glad. Remember how he talked of preparing for the down slope every time the top of success was reached? I am glad God took him at the top of his success."

Again we were silent as Gen. Gay turned his chair around to face me, saying, "The longer I am in the States, the happier I am that the General never returned to see our society as it is today."

A secretary came in for the third time to say that they had people holding on the telephone for Gen. Gay. I left the room. I should have saluted, but we did not speak because we were both crying.

It was my good fortune to visit with Gen. Gay in El Paso a year before his death. At the time, Gen. Gay was in the hospital from a fall on slippery sidewalk.

We "refought" the war and our experiences together. Gen. Gay's memory of Gen. Patton's death was exactly the same as he had reported in Chicago. My memories of Gen. Patton and his principles have influenced my life. Twice I have been sentenced to death by doctors for bone cancer. At such times I remembered Gen. Patton's words, "Live until you die! Death will be more exciting than life. If you can take death, you can enjoy

231

life! Death is only a phase in the cycle of life."

Many times I have followed his principles and turned away from feuds in politics, church, and family because "nothing would have been gained by winning."

I fought some battles with government officials who failed to remember that the people of the United States are sovereign; not political leaders. To use a Gen. Patton quote, "I killed a few skunks in the government who were digging under the front porch of our house, The Constitution."

When I won a battle I was ready to be attacked, remembering Gen. Patton's advice, "When you are on top there is no place to go but down."

I treasure the hours I spent with Gen. Patton. I remember his asking me if I had to hate a man to prosecute him in court for some criminal act. We agreed that in combat in war or combat in the courts, we had the duty to do what had to be done whether with hate or without hate. We discussed how necessary it would be to find a way to turn men off from killing when the war was over. I remember his saying, "It may be harder to turn our fine American young men into peace-loving citizens than it is to turn them into killers."

HISTORY WILL GIVE HIM
TRIBUTES FOREVER

World War II needed a commander who understood the nature of war; who knew that war meant killing people. Gen. Patton was that commander. For Gen. Patton, war would never be a political battle, a cure for unemployment, a chance for political office, or a way to help the economy. War meant that people had to be killed to have peace. The quicker the enemy could be killed, the quicker the war would be over.

The war with Germany ended when Hitler knew he would be captured and killed. Hitler died from self-destruction; his own self-discipline.

The war with Japan ended when the atomic bomb made certain that all of the leaders of Japan could be killed. The atomic bomb brought peace. Such a bomb can bring peace when those starting the war know they can be killed when the first bomb explodes.

I am sure Gen. Patton would accept any such weapon of total destruction just as man accepted and made good use of fire, the long spear, and machine guns.

I am sure Gen. Patton would say, "If God had not wanted the nuclear bomb, He would not have helped man invent it!"

Gen. Patton will receive the tributes which he deserves from the historians of the world. The Patton movie is used to instill courage in the White House, to build spirit in football teams, and to inspire military cadets.

A high tribute was given to Gen. Patton by British Gen. H. Essame who said, "He personified the national genius which raised the United States from humble beginnings to a world power."

Gen. Essame also wrote, "Gen. Patton wanted to

win in the shortest possible time. Never in the history of the world is there an instance of a single army having such a great effect in deciding the major issues of a campaign. Third Army's record is peerless by any measure." A great tribute from a great British general!

Gen. Patton accomplished his victories despite all of the reprimands for advancing against orders and the refusal of the high commands to supply his troops with fuel for attacks for easy victories. Gen. Patton bounced from the bottom every time to win the war for those who wanted to stop his rapid advances to defeat the enemy.

Gen. Patton's most effective weapon was not the armored tank. It was the individual soldier who was trained to be completely fearless. In truth, as Gen. Patton said so often, "Every American soldier is a four-star army." Gen. Patton's soldiers learned to love the thrill of facing death in combat. They followed Gen. Patton's principle that the greatest thrill of life was the ability to face death. For him combat with the enemy meant an end to the killing of people on both sides. If he had been permitted to pursue the defeated enemy, the war would have been over many months earlier.

Major General H. Essame also wrote, "Gen. Patton had opportunities which he was not permitted to follow - which would have proven decisive, shortened the war, saved thousands of lives, and left the West in a better strategic posture than it would be more than a quarter of a century later."

Gen. Essame's book about Gen. Patton is entitled, A STUDY IN COMMAND.

Gen. Essame's evaluation of Gen. Patton was confirmed by the German General, Richard Schimpf, who said, "We always confidently relied on Allied hesitancy to exploit successes to give us time to withdraw and regroup in order to slow up the next thrust. But with your Gen. Patton, it was different! He was very aggressive in exploiting a penetration. His break through at Avranches was an outstanding example of this. So was his phenomenal campaign in the Palatinate. There is no question if your Third Army had not been halted before Metz in September, it could have penetrated the Siegfried Line very quickly and been on the Rhine in a short time. At that time we were powerless to cope with the situation in that portion of the front. But when your Third Army was halted, we obtained the time to regroup, and we used it to the utmost!"

Gen. Patton is buried in Luxembourg with his troops with the same cross as every other soldier. The crosses give the name, rank, serial number, and organization of the soldiers. Gen. Patton's cross states, "Geo. S. Patton, Jr., General. 02605. 3rd Army." Nothing on the cross indicates that he was the Commanding General. He would want it that way. He is serving with his men and not over them.

Several times his grave has been moved to a larger area because so many were visiting his grave that the grass and grave markers of the other soldiers were damaged. The governments involved in this change could never get permission from Gen. Patton to move his grave away from the soldiers! I am sure God was scolded in no uncertain terms for permitting the grave to be moved.

Years after his death I talked with Gen. Patton's son and daughter about moving their father's grave to the United States. They replied, "We have discussed this many times with the family. The grave site cannot be changed."

History Will Give Him
Tributes Forever

Although it was Gen. Patton's wish to be with his soldiers, I regret that the "greatest military commander" of our history is on foreign soil.

In talking with the daughter, I asked, "I knew your father and mother wanted to buried in the same grave. Is it possible . . ."

Before I could finish she said, "Somehow, I know they are together someplace!"

All of Gen. Patton's principles came pouring into my mind when I was driving alone on an interstate highway in Oklahoma. By some quirk in the clouds and radio waves, I was receiving a radio station from Seattle, Washington. The radio announcer was interviewing a descendent of the Indian Chief, Seattle. The words of the Indian Chief were so close to Gen. Patton's principles that I quickly wrote the words on a map as the descendent spoke. When I repeated the words I could see that Gen. Patton had packed the wisdom of the centuries into the principles which he gave to the troops.

The descendent of Chief Seattle quoted his ancestor, "There is no death, only a change of life. The dead are not powerless!"

Gen. Patton is not dead! He has had a change in the phase of his life!

His principles will have power forever.

INDEX

Index

Index

Index

Index

Index

Index

ACKNOWLEDGMENTS

I acknowledge appreciation to so many for the encouragement to write this book.

To Gen. Patton's daughter, Ruth Ellen, for facts and for her endorsement, "Your book is the best about my father."

To Gen. Patton's son for his review and comment, "My Dad would be proud to have his principles sorted out by you."

To the lady who came to me after my luncheon address for a Tucson club who said, "Thank you for giving Gen. Patton's ideas about death. I will always remember the words, 'Death is only a phase in the cycle of life.' I buried my husband last week. I can go on with my life now!"

To Dr. Joe Bettridge, Pastor, St. Andrews Presbyterian Church, Tucson, Arizona - for the quotation, "when sins abound."

To the editors of the South Bend Tribune, for the information about the soldier slapped by Gen. Patton.

Photo credits to the following:
Major Gen. George S. Patton, III, the son of Gen. Patton.

Kay Durban for photographs and confirmation of the black shield for Benedict Arnold at our West Point Military Academy.

The Department of the Army, The Pentagon.

Special appreciation to my wonderful wife and son for giving me so much to live for through military and surgical tours of duty in addition to the "tour of duty" of writing this book.

Porter B. Williamson

NOTES